100 JOBS IN ESPORTS

A CAREER PLANNING BOOK BY COACH ALNE ACADEMY
IN COLLABORATION WITH HITMARKER.NET

Coach Alne Academy

SCAN ME

Hitmarker.net

SCAN ME

This book wouldn't have been possible without the support of Hitmarker.net

Hitmarker is the #1 resource for jobs in the video game industry. They provided all of the data needed to create this book and ensure its accuracy.

You can use the QR code below to create a free account with Hitmarker and start exploring the real job opportunities in esports that this book is based on.

Thank you again to Hitmarker.net.

100 JOBS IN ESPORTS

COVER DESIGN BY HITMARKER.NET

ISBN: 979-8-9872773-0-0 (Hardback)
ISBN: 979-8-9872773-1-7 (Paperback)
ISBN: 979-8-9872773-2-4 (Student Edition)

BE READY TO SCAN QR CODES:

QR codes are used throughout this book to provide additional resources. These will be maintained by the authors and updated when necessary, which means your book will remain full of modern, relevant information! We hope you take advantage of the QR codes provided to expand your learning.

 SCAN ME

PAY ATTENTION TO THE EXPERIENCE:

Each job page contains a bar indicating the level of experience required for that job. If you're just starting out in your career, focus on the entry and junior level positions. You can always see how these jobs might progress in the future by looking at the 'roles this job could unlock' heading on each page. Ideally, you want to find a job you'd enjoy at each experience level. Then you can start building towards your dream career path in esports.

Entry   Junior   Inter.   Senior

LOOK FOR CLUES ON EACH PAGE:

Each job page has a useful index at the bottom indicating whether it requires a college degree or not, as well as pointing you in the direction of similar jobs you might be interested in!

Don't like this job?   Like this job?   May require a college degree

READ AS YOU LIKE:

You may read front-to-back but it's not required. This book has been designed for you to flip through, search around and plan your career from.

TABLE OF CONTENTS:

INTRODUCTION

Hey Coach, I want to learn about jobs in esports as I have always loved competing. I spend all of my free time playing scrims, tournaments and even signed up for my high school esports team! I would love to work in esports one day but I don't know how to get started. Can you help?

Of course! Esports is still very new and can be confusing at times. Luckily, you have come to the right place. To begin with, we'll need to do some digging to figure out what jobs might interest you, since there are over 100 different jobs in esports that all require different skills.

Wow, I had no idea there were so many jobs to choose from! Do you really think we can find the right job for me? I'm not even sure what I should be looking for.

No problem! We'll begin by taking a personality test to find the first job I think you will like. Then, I'll recommend another role depending on if you liked that job or not. We should be able to build a full career plan this way, starting with an entry level job and ending with a senior position!

CONTINUE TO PERSONALITY TEST

PERSONALITY TEST

SCAN ME

MEET YOUR PROFESSORS

JEREMY **COACH** **OLIVER** **KELLY**

SHAUN **BURNS**

REED **VICTORIA** **DOOR**

TEAM OPERATIONS & COMPETITION INTRO

TEAM OPERATIONS & COMPETITION

Working in esports has always been my passion, but if I don't go pro I'm not sure what options I have. I love the competitive scene and traveling to tournaments. Is it possible to have a career where I'm still involved in esports without actually competing?

Actually, there are more opportunities to work for a team than there are to play for one! A whole range of expertise is needed for an organization to operate successfully, so while the players do take center stage, their achievements are made possible by an entire staff behind the scenes.

That makes a lot of sense! I guess I never thought about it that way before. Do the staff members really play that big of a role in helping their players win championships?

Absolutely! Think about it: players compete for up to 8-12 hours a day to stay competitive. With so little free time, they need support. This is where staff in the competitive sector come in. Let's take a look at some of the jobs now...

CONTINUE TO JOBS 1-1

TEAM ANALYST

As a Team Analyst, you'll be responsible for collecting and analyzing data on both your team and competitive rivals. You'll use this information to support your players and fellow coaches with insights, conclusions and what to expect during official matches. A good team analyst can use data to highlight weaknesses in an opposing side, while also advising their own players where they can improve. As such, you'll need to be a true expert in your game of choice and have a background working with numbers to secure a job in this field.

EXPERIENCE LEVEL:

Entry   Junior   Inter.   Senior

ROLES THIS JOB COULD UNLOCK:

- Head Coach
- Desk Analyst

ADDITIONAL RESOURCE:

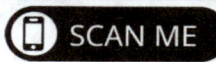 SCAN ME

ROLES THAT LEAD INTO THIS JOB:

- Data Analyst
- Assistant Coach

KEY RESPONSIBILITIES:

- Conducting research on opposing sides
- Creating data-driven insights to support your team
- Identifying where individual players could improve through data

KEY REQUIREMENTS:

- Bachelor's degree in statistics, mathematics or similar a plus
- Experience in coaching or a supporting staff role
- Proficiency with SQL, Excel or a similar tool/language

Don't like this job?
Try page 60

Like this job?
Try page 16

May require a college degree

Don't like this job? Try page 60

Like this job? Try page 16

TEAM OPERATIONS & COMPETITION

TEAM SCOUT

As a Team Scout, you'll be responsible for discovering up-and-coming esports players and signing them to your org. A good scout has the instinct and game knowledge needed to spot rising stars early. For this reason, you must be well-connected in your game's community to succeed. You'll need to be willing to immerse yourself in its competitive scene, attending tournaments and paying close attention to its path-to-pro system. You'll then deliver scouting reports to your organization to help them select future players.

EXPERIENCE LEVEL:

Entry	Junior	Inter.	Senior

ROLES THIS JOB COULD UNLOCK:

- Team Coach
- Team Manager

ADDITIONAL RESOURCE:

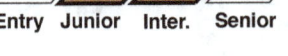

SCAN ME

ROLES THAT LEAD INTO THIS JOB:

- Amateur Coach
- Amateur/Pro Player

KEY RESPONSIBILITIES:

- Delivering scouting reports to coaching staff
- Identifying potential new player signings
- Maintaining a detailed overview of the amateur/semi-pro level

KEY REQUIREMENTS:

- An active presence in the esports community
- Expert game knowledge
- Prior experience as an amateur coach or player

Don't like this job?
Try page 22

Like this job?
Try page 16

Does not require a college degree

TEAM OPERATIONS & COMPETITION

PERFORMANCE COACH

As a Performance Coach, you'll be responsible for the physical and mental well-being of your team. It'll be your job to develop a conditioning plan, workout routine and mental fortitude programs to support players in all aspects of their game. In some cases, you will also be in charge of substance abuse monitoring for the FDA or specific leagues, like the LCS. A good performance coach puts their players' well-being at the forefront, identifying any mental health struggles or burnout early so they can be addressed appropriately.

EXPERIENCE LEVEL:

Entry | Junior | Inter. | Senior

ROLES THIS JOB COULD UNLOCK:

- Head of Performance
- Performance Coach (sports)

ADDITIONAL RESOURCE:

 SCAN ME

ROLES THAT LEAD INTO THIS JOB:

- Performance Coordinator (sports)
- Strength & Conditioning Coach (sports)

KEY RESPONSIBILITIES:

- Developing conditioning plans for each player
- Providing mental support during matches
- Working alongside coaching staff to unlock each player's full potenti

KEY REQUIREMENTS:

- Bachelor's degree in sports science, physical education or health scie
- Certifications in nutrition or personal training a plus
- Prior experience as an athlete, professional trainer or sports coach

Don't like this job?
Try page 47

Like this job?
Try page 76

Requires a college degree

TEAM OPERATIONS COMPETITIO

TEAM CHEF

As a Team Chef, you'll be responsible for preparing meals for your team. This will typically be two meals per day for at least five days per week, so it is a full time job, with the chef also managing the monthly food budget. A team chef will often be asked to prioritize one cuisine in particular, since esports orgs recruit from all over the world and serving their players familiar food can help them feel comfortable in their new environment. Nutrition and competitive performance also go hand-in-hand, which makes a chef that much more important!

EXPERIENCE LEVEL:

Entry Junior Inter. Senior

ROLES THIS JOB COULD UNLOCK:

- Head Chef
- Nutritional Advisor

ADDITIONAL RESOURCE:

 SCAN ME

ROLES THAT LEAD INTO THIS JOB:

- Chef
- Line Cook

KEY RESPONSIBILITIES:

- Cooking authentic, worldwide cuisine for players
- Keeping the house well-stocked with ingredients and snacks
- Planning, preparing and serving 2+ meals each day

KEY REQUIREMENTS:

- Experience cooking for large groups
- Knowledge of multicultural cuisines and specialties
- Professional culinary training

Don't like this job?
Try page 28

Like this job?
Try page 50

May require a college degree

TEAM OPERATIONS & COMPETITION

15

TEAM COACH

As a Team Coach, you'll be responsible for the development, coordination and growth of your esports team. This includes organizing practices and working with your players to improve teamwork, communication and decision-making. Coaches can not normally talk to the team during official matches, which means a good coach must build their players up to be leaders themselves, capable of executing their game plan when it matters. As you might expect, a background in the semi-pro or pro esports scene is almost essential to this role.

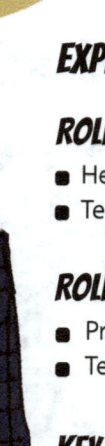

EXPERIENCE LEVEL:

Entry   Junior   **Inter.**   **Senior**

ROLES THIS JOB COULD UNLOCK:

- Head of Esports
- Team Manager

ROLES THAT LEAD INTO THIS JOB:

- Professional Player
- Team Analyst

ADDITIONAL RESOURCE:

 SCAN ME

KEY RESPONSIBILITIES:

- Analyzing game play and preparing strategies for your team
- Coaching players pre and post-game to help them win
- Serving as a leader and always putting the team's needs first

KEY REQUIREMENTS:

- 1+ years as an assistant coach or analyst at the pro level
- Best-in-class game knowledge
- Experience as a professional player a plus

Don't like this job?
Try page 56

Like this job?
Try page 17

May require a college degree

TEAM OPERATIONS & COMPETITION

TEAM MANAGER

As a Team Manager, you'll be responsible for the day-to-day operations of your esports team. This includes managing player schedules, fulfilling sponsor deliverables and acting as a bridge between the team and your organization's management. A good team manager handles the finer details of travel and business operations so the players can focus on one goal: bringing home championships!

EXPERIENCE LEVEL:

Entry   Junior   Inter.   Senior

ROLES THIS JOB COULD UNLOCK:

- General Manager
- Head of Esports

ADDITIONAL RESOURCE:

 SCAN ME

ROLES THAT LEAD INTO THIS JOB:

- Pro Player
- Team Coach

KEY RESPONSIBILITIES:

- Acting as your team's point-of-contact for all external companies
- Eliminating stresses from players and coaching staff
- Managing the team's schedule and commitments

KEY REQUIREMENTS:

- 2+ years as a pro player, analyst or team coach
- Bachelor's degree in business management or equivalent experience
- Being highly organized, dependable and professional in your work

Don't like this job? Try page 89

Like this job? Try page 18

May require a college degree

TEAM OPERATIONS & COMPETITION

GENERAL MANAGER

As a General Manager, you'll be responsible for the entire esports division of your organization. You will work closely with team managers, coaching staff and league operators of each game that your org is active in, with your goal being both success in the server and in your business. It's a high-level position that requires significant experience in the esports industry and management in general.

EXPERIENCE LEVEL:

Entry	Junior	Inter.	Senior

ROLES THIS JOB COULD UNLOCK:

- Chief Gaming Officer
- VP of Esports

ROLES THAT LEAD INTO THIS JOB:

- Team Coach
- Team Manager

ADDITIONAL RESOURCE:

 SCAN ME

KEY RESPONSIBILITIES:

- Ensuring smooth day-to-day operations within your organization
- Guiding coaching staff to deliver championships
- Overseeing financials and business performance

KEY REQUIREMENTS:

- 3+ years in esports management
- Advanced understanding of the esports industry
- Background in people or project management

Don't like this job? Try page 94

Like this job? Try page 51

May require a college degree

TEAM OPERATIONS & COMPETITION

CONTINUE TO CONTENT AND MARKETING

CONTENT AND MARKETING

I spend a lot of time watching creators online. I even started making my own content and follow all of the big esports teams on social media. I would love to work in online content but I don't have a large following, is it still possible?

Of course! Being a well-known creator isn't the only way to make a career out of your creativity — there are so many other options. I'm sure we can find you a job that doesn't require a follower count.

That's awesome! I enjoy making content but I do it as a hobby more than anything. I'm not sure what job it could lead to. Should I even be spending my time on it or should I focus on something else?

Creating content can absolutely develop the skills you'll need to find a job in this field, but it's rarely a hard requirement. You're in the right section if you have that creative urge, though, so let's check out some of your options…

CONTINUE TO JOBS 8-20

SOCIAL MEDIA MANAGER

As a Social Media Manager, you'll be taking control of your brand's social media pages. These are a crucial marketing channel in the esports industry and utilized by companies of all sizes. While it can sometimes be seen as an 'easier' job than others, you won't simply be posting Tweets. You'll also be pipelining content weeks in advance, working on marketing strategy and engaging with your community. It also helps to have basic photo and video editing skills, though you'll typically have a content team to assist you here.

EXPERIENCE LEVEL:

Entry   Junior   Inter.   Senior

ROLES THIS JOB COULD UNLOCK:

- Head of Social Media
- Marketing Manager

ADDITIONAL RESOURCE:

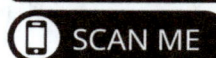 SCAN ME

ROLES THAT LEAD INTO THIS JOB:

- Freelance Content Creator/Writer
- Social Media Intern

KEY RESPONSIBILITIES:

- Brainstorming content for a variety of channels
- Engaging with your community through replies, likes and stories
- Generating data reports to monitor your performance

KEY REQUIREMENTS:

- Background in running social media or fan pages
- Deeply tapped into online and social trends
- Experience in creative writing, graphic or video editing a plus

Don't like this job?
Try page 60

Like this job?
Try page 29

May require a college degree

CONTENT & MARKETING

GRAPHIC DESIGNER

As a Graphic Designer, you'll be responsible for upholding your company's visual identity. You'll do this through designing social media graphics, thumbnails, website assets and more. Graphic designers in esports don't always work a traditional 9-5 shift pattern, as organizations need to be reactive when their team is competing, which is often on the weekend. As a result, the best graphic designers will automate as much of this as possible by creating templates that a social media manager can edit.

EXPERIENCE LEVEL:

Entry   Junior   Inter.   Senior

ROLES THIS JOB COULD UNLOCK:

- Creative Director
- Head of Design

ADDITIONAL RESOURCE:

SCAN ME

ROLES THAT LEAD INTO THIS JOB:

- Freelance Designer
- Graphic Design Intern

KEY RESPONSIBILITIES:

- Assisting colleagues with graphics upon request
- Creating visuals to support social media posts
- Helping define the company's brand and visual identity

KEY REQUIREMENTS:

- 1+ years of experience in the Adobe Suite or similar
- Professional or freelance design experience
- Strong portfolio of work that's ready to share

**Don't like this job?
Try page 83**

**Like this job?
Try page 63**

May require a college degree

CONTENT & MARKETING

VIDEO EDITOR

As a Video Editor, you'll be responsible for taking raw video footage and bringing it to life. You'll work with producers, videographers and creative directors to create stunning visuals for your brand. Being a good video editor is more than simply knowing how to use video editing programs; you must be able to tell a cohesive story that grips viewers. This means learning how to use color grading, sound design and voice clips effectively to create stand-out pieces of content.

EXPERIENCE LEVEL:

Entry   Junior   Inter.   Senior

ROLES THIS JOB COULD UNLOCK:

- Creative Director
- Head of Production

ADDITIONAL RESOURCE:

 SCAN ME

ROLES THAT LEAD INTO THIS JOB:

- Freelance Editor
- Video Editing Intern

KEY RESPONSIBILITIES:

- Creating clip content for social media
- Editing longer-form content for YouTube and sponsor deliverables
- Responding to other company video requests as required

KEY REQUIREMENTS:

- 1+ years working in Premiere Pro or similar
- A portfolio of diverse video editing examples
- Exceptional storytelling ability

Don't like this job?
Try page 54

Like this job?
Try page 34

May require a college degree

CONTENT & MARKETING

PRESENTER/HOST

As a Presenter or Channel Host, you'll be responsible for recording highly engaging videos with the content team, often becoming the face for a brand or video network. This role is regularly offered to junior candidates on a freelance basis, making it an ideal starting point to build your on-camera showreel. If you're interested in this area, you should focus on mastering your subject topic, how to project your voice and professional breathing techniques. A good presenter can grow into a number of roles in the entertainment industry.

EXPERIENCE LEVEL:

Entry   Junior   Inter.   Senior

ROLES THIS JOB COULD UNLOCK:

- Content Creator
- Desk Host

ADDITIONAL RESOURCE:

 SCAN ME

ROLES THAT LEAD INTO THIS JOB:

- Amatuer Caster/On-Air Talent
- Freelance Video Producer

KEY RESPONSIBILITIES:

- Conducting interviews with players and industry personalities
- Delivering engaging on-camera performances
- Supporting the content team with video ideas

KEY REQUIREMENTS:

- A portfolio of on-camera work (even if self-produced)
- Confident, outgoing personality
- Some knowledge of pacing, delivery and breathing techniques

**Don't like this job?
Try page 77**

**Like this job?
Try page 57**

Does not require a college degree

CONTENT & MARKETING

VIDEOGRAPHER

As a Videographer, you'll be responsible for collecting video footage for your organization. You'll work with producers and creative directors to collect all of the material needed to create memorable documentaries and other content. More than most esports jobs, this role is likely to involve a significant amount of travel, so you'll need to be comfortable with this as well as filming in a variety of different environments. You should understand how the likes of lighting, composition and audio shape your end product, along with what equipment is suitable to use in each recording session.

EXPERIENCE LEVEL:

Entry   Junior   Inter.   Senior

ROLES THIS JOB COULD UNLOCK:
- Creative Director
- Head of Production

ADDITIONAL RESOURCE:

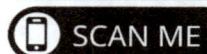 SCAN ME

ROLES THAT LEAD INTO THIS JOB:
- Freelance Videographer
- Videography Intern

KEY RESPONSIBILITIES:
- Capturing video footage of your organization's activities
- Cataloging your files so that they're easy to access
- Traveling, often internationally, to film your team wherever they are

KEY REQUIREMENTS:
- 1+ years of recording video footage
- Ability to film in a range of environments
- Exceptional storytelling ability

Don't like this job?
Try page 84

Like this job?
Try page 60

May require a college degree

CONTENT & MARKETING

COMMUNITY MANAGER

As a Community Manager, you'll be responsible for developing an active and engaged community around your brand. This role is similar to that of a social media manager, but with a greater focus on community retention, social listening and online events. If a social media manager attracts people to a brand, then a community manager keeps them invested after joining. If you love talking to people about gaming, esports and pop culture, this might be the job for you.

EXPERIENCE LEVEL:

Entry **Junior** **Inter.** **Senior**

ROLES THIS JOB COULD UNLOCK:
- Head of Social Media
- Marketing Manager

ROLES THAT LEAD INTO THIS JOB:
- Discord Moderator
- Social Media Intern

ADDITIONAL RESOURCE:

 SCAN ME

KEY RESPONSIBILITIES:
- Engaging community members through social media and live events
- Generating reports on community sentiment towards your brand
- Serving as a bridge between a company and its community

KEY REQUIREMENTS:
- Deep understanding of social media and online trends
- Expertise in Discord and its bots
- Strong written communication and data analysis skills

Don't like this job? Try page 128

Like this job? Try page 29

May require a college degree

CONTENT & MARKETING

CONTENT COORDINATOR

As a Content Coordinator, you'll be responsible for tracking the content your organization produces and distributing it on the correct channels. You will work on both internal content projects for your organization as well as sponsor deliverables, with a focus on making sure deadlines are hit and assisting in the production process whenever needed. This is a multi-purpose role that combines social media, video production and marketing into one.

EXPERIENCE LEVEL:

Entry   Junior   Inter.   Senior

ROLES THIS JOB COULD UNLOCK:

- Head of Content
- Marketing Manager

ADDITIONAL RESOURCE:

 SCAN ME

ROLES THAT LEAD INTO THIS JOB:

- Junior Video Editor
- Social Media Assistant

KEY RESPONSIBILITIES:

- Coordinating with colleagues and partners on content deliverables
- Ideating new content campaigns
- Responding to ad hoc tasks such as creating website content

KEY REQUIREMENTS:

- Excellent written and verbal communication
- Familiar with the Adobe Suite and video production
- Substantial knowledge of social media and online trends

Don't like this job?
Try page 102

Like this job?
Try page 116

May require a college degree

CONTENT & MARKETING

MARKETING MANAGER

As a Marketing Manager, you'll be responsible for growing the reach of your organization and its products. You'll participate in brainstorming sessions to come up with ideas and then work with the relevant teams to put these into motion. This role merges the creativity of content creation and social media with a more data-driven approach. A good marketing manager is imaginative, business-savvy and capable of amplifying their company's message through organic and paid promotions.

EXPERIENCE LEVEL:

Entry	Junior	Inter.	Senior

ROLES THIS JOB COULD UNLOCK:

- Creative Director
- Head of Marketing

ADDITIONAL RESOURCE:

 SCAN ME

ROLES THAT LEAD INTO THIS JOB:

- Community Manager
- Social Media Manager

KEY RESPONSIBILITIES:

- Developing marketing strategies that suit your target audience
- Generating reports to evaluate a campaign's success
- Making regular changes to paid campaigns to optimize performance

KEY REQUIREMENTS:

- 2+ years working in marketing, creative or social media
- Excellent understanding of the esports industry and fanbase
- Impeccable written communication and data analysis skills

Don't like this job? Try page 88

Like this job? Try page 72

Requires a college degree

CONTENT & MARKETING

TALENT MANAGER

As a Talent Manager, you'll be in charge of working with content creators at an organization, brand or talent agency. The focus of the job is to coordinate any marketing campaigns that involve the talent under your umbrella. Good talent managers handle the admin and scheduling tasks for creators, while also seeking out new sponsorship deals for them to take part in. On top of this, you might also be tasked with signing new creators to be represented by your company.

EXPERIENCE LEVEL:

Entry	Junior	Inter.	Senior
	■	■	

ROLES THIS JOB COULD UNLOCK:

- Head of Talent
- Influencer Marketing Manager

ROLES THAT LEAD INTO THIS JOB:

- Content Creator
- Talent Coordinator

ADDITIONAL RESOURCE:

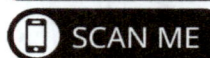
SCAN ME

KEY RESPONSIBILITIES:

- Building relationships with talent and industry partners
- Organizing and project-managing influencer campaigns
- Overseeing talent during on-site events

KEY REQUIREMENTS:

- Account management or customer success experience
- Expert knowledge across Twitch, YouTube and social media
- Prior experience as a content creator a plus

Don't like this job?
Try page 50

Like this job?
Try page 62

May require a college degree

CONTENT & MARKETING

APPAREL DESIGNER

As an Apparel Designer, you'll be responsible for designing new clothing lines for your organization. You will build concepts that fit your brand's identity, before realizing them by selecting materials and other production details . This role partners closely with an organization's creative director and marketing manager to ensure that each collection carries the right message. An understanding of the business side of apparel is crucial, too, in order to keep products commercially viable.

EXPERIENCE LEVEL:

Entry   Junior   Inter.   Senior

ROLES THIS JOB COULD UNLOCK:

- Creative Director
- Head of Apparel

ADDITIONAL RESOURCE:

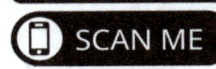
SCAN ME

ROLES THAT LEAD INTO THIS JOB:

- Graphic Designer
- Graphic Design Intern

KEY RESPONSIBILITIES:

- Designing new apparel collections
- Ensuring collections stay within budget and on schedule
- Reviewing sample products throughout the manufacturing process

KEY REQUIREMENTS:

- 2+ years in graphic or apparel design (or a combination of the two)
- A portfolio of work featuring a variety of clothing designs
- Knowledge of how apparel is manufactured

Don't like this job? Try page 64

Like this job? Try page 34

May require a college degree

CONTENT & MARKETING

PAID MEDIA MANAGER

As a Paid Media Manager, you'll be responsible for running digital advertising campaigns. This is a marketing role that's usually only hired for by larger companies, due to it having a specific focus on display, search and video adverts. You'll use services like Google Ads or ad agencies to set up campaigns where you pay per impression, click or conversion. Ultimately, your goal is to drive new business to the company for the lowest spend possible.

EXPERIENCE LEVEL:

Entry	Junior	Inter.	Senior

ROLES THIS JOB COULD UNLOCK:

- Head of Digital Marketing
- Marketing Director

ADDITIONAL RESOURCE:

 SCAN ME

ROLES THAT LEAD INTO THIS JOB:

- Digital Marketing Specialist
- Junior Campaign Manager

KEY RESPONSIBILITIES:

- Creating digital marketing campaigns and monitoring performance
- Maintaining relationships with ad partners and agencies
- Seeking out new channels to advertise on

KEY REQUIREMENTS:

- Analytical, data-driven mindset
- Comfortable writing advertising copy
- Experience in digital marketing or paid social

Don't like this job?
Try page 104

Like this job?
Try page 48

Requires a college degree

CONTENT & MARKETING

SEO MANAGER

As an SEO Manager, you'll be responsible for optimizing company websites for searchability. Organic search traffic—from engines like Google and Bing—is immensely valuable, and SEO managers work to get their website as high up the results page as possible for search terms that are relevant to them. This means auditing how SEO-friendly a website is and conducting outreach to increase its authority. A good SEO manager will be analytical, familiar with web content and possess a strong understanding of how search engines order their results.

EXPERIENCE LEVEL:

Entry Junior **Inter.** Senior

ROLES THIS JOB COULD UNLOCK:

- Head of Marketing
- Marketing Manager

ROLES THAT LEAD INTO THIS JOB:

- Content Writer
- Digital Marketing Coordinator

ADDITIONAL RESOURCE:

 SCAN ME

KEY RESPONSIBILITIES:

- Auditing the company website(s) to ensure they're optimized for SEO
- Conducting keyword research to find high-value terms to rank for
- Performing website and PR outreach to build new backlinks

KEY REQUIREMENTS:

- 2+ years working in digital or paid marketing
- Maintaining an in-depth knowledge of SEO best practices
- Strong written and verbal communication

Don't like this job?
Try page 12

Like this job?
Try page 122

Requires a college degree

CONTENT & MARKETING

CREATIVE DIRECTOR

As a Creative Director, you'll be responsible for defining your brand's identity. You'll manage a company's creative department and set the standards for how visual and graphical content should be presented. Creative directors are a senior part of an organization and play a major role in how the brand is perceived online. While an understanding of esports is important in this job, preference is given to candidates with a stellar track record in the creative field — even if that's not within esports.

EXPERIENCE LEVEL:

Entry	Junior	Inter.	Senior
			■

ROLES THIS JOB COULD UNLOCK:

- Chief Content Officer
- Chief Marketing Officer

ADDITIONAL RESOURCE:

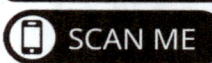
SCAN ME

ROLES THAT LEAD INTO THIS JOB:

- Graphic Designer
- Marketing Manager

KEY RESPONSIBILITIES:

- Defining brand guidelines and identity
- Mentoring members of the creative team
- Using creative content to achieve your company's business goals

KEY REQUIREMENTS:

- 5+ years working in content production or marketing
- Experience managing a team
- Solid understanding of how to engage the esports community

Don't like this job?
Try page 51

Like this job?
Try page 123

May require a college degree

CONTENT & MARKETING

CONTINUE TO JOURNALISM AND WRITING

JOURNALISM AND WRITING

I've always enjoyed writing but never really thought about how I could use that to work in esports. I thought I would have to write novels or work for a newspaper and I didn't know if I would find that interesting enough.

Well luckily for you, the esports industry is full of opportunties for writers! Just like any other industry, there is a huge demand for covering news, events and pop culture. Writers can work for esports teams, publishers and websites.

That sounds like fun, but I'm not sure how to get started. Should I write blog posts about video games, or is there a better way to stand out from the crowd?

Well, it depends on what kind of writer you would like to become! There are a number of different writing styles and jobs to choose from so let's start by narrowing down which sounds the most interesting to you…

CONTINUE TO JOBS 21-25

COPYWRITER

As a Copywriter, you'll be responsible for producing marketing copy across your company's channels. This could be for social media posts, landing pages, email blasts and advertisements. Unlike other writing roles, this position has a core requirement of having a marketing background. As such, you'll need to be able to write snappy, compelling copy as well as understand marketing principles like A/B testing and how to optimize your copy to generate the highest number of conversions. The best copywriters are able to communicate a complex message in only a handful of words.

EXPERIENCE LEVEL:

Entry　Junior　Inter.　Senior

ROLES THIS JOB COULD UNLOCK:
- Editor
- Marketing Manager

ADDITIONAL RESOURCE:

ROLES THAT LEAD INTO THIS JOB:
- Marketing Coordinator
- Paid Media Manager

SCAN ME

KEY RESPONSIBILITIES:
- Producing copy for all of your company's channels
- Utilizing A/B tests to understand what copy converts best
- Writing copy that sells products and captures interest

KEY REQUIREMENTS:
- A portfolio of written work with a clear specialism in advertising cop
- Internship or experience within a marketing agency a plus
- Outstanding written ability and an understanding of marketing

Don't like this job?
Try page 70

Like this job?
Try page 29

May require a college degree

JOURNALISM & WRITING

NEWS WRITER

As a News Writer, you'll be responsible for covering news stories across esports. As a fast-paced industry, being able to provide readers with the full story in a timely manner is incredibly important, meaning there's more to this role than 'simply writing'. A good news writer will be wired into the esports scene, with personal relationships they can draw on to support stories when possible. An understanding of journalistic ethics is crucial, too, which is something you should look into if you've not studied the field formally.

EXPERIENCE LEVEL:

Entry   Junior   Inter.   Senior

ROLES THIS JOB COULD UNLOCK:

- Editor
- Senior Writer

ADDITIONAL RESOURCE:

 SCAN ME

ROLES THAT LEAD INTO THIS JOB:

- Freelance Writer
- Independent Journalist/Writer

KEY RESPONSIBILITIES:

- Actively monitoring your area of coverage
- Building relationships within the industry to acquire exclusive stories
- Seeking out relevant news stories to report on

KEY REQUIREMENTS:

- A portfolio of written work (including self-published articles)
- Bachelor's degree in journalism or creative writing a plus
- Flawless written communication

Don't like this job?
Try page 102

Like this job?
Try page 42

May require a college degree

JOURNALISM & WRITING

FEATURES WRITER

As a Features Writer, you'll be responsible for writing long-form feature articles. Feature writers can really flex their creativity in the way they present their stories, which might be centered around the rise and fall of a certain player, the importance of an upcoming tournament or something more niche. Many jobs in this field are offered on a freelance basis. It is still possible to build a career in, though, as prolific esports feature writers can go on to establish large personal brands through their work.

EXPERIENCE LEVEL:

Entry	Junior	Inter.	Senior

ROLES THIS JOB COULD UNLOCK:

- Content Creator
- Editor

ADDITIONAL RESOURCE:

 SCAN ME

ROLES THAT LEAD INTO THIS JOB:

- News Writer
- Video Content Creator

KEY RESPONSIBILITIES:

- Pitching unique feature ideas to your editor
- Sourcing industry figures to support articles with quotes
- Writing evergreen, SEO-focused articles

KEY REQUIREMENTS:

- A portfolio of written work (including self-published articles)
- Creative, with the ability to spot interesting story angles
- Flawless written communication

Don't like this job?
Try page 82

Like this job?
Try page 42

May require a college degree

JOURNALISM & WRITING

PR MANAGER

As a PR Manager, you'll be responsible for shaping your company's public image. You'll work closely with members of the media by distributing press releases, seeking to generate coverage and responding to comment requests. PR managers in esports also play a big role at live events by helping members of the press set up interviews with players and, ultimately, increase the reach of that event and its sponsors. This is a role that blends journalism, writing and marketing into one.

EXPERIENCE LEVEL:

Entry | Junior | Inter. | Senior

ROLES THIS JOB COULD UNLOCK:

- Head of Communications
- Marketing Director

ADDITIONAL RESOURCE:

ROLES THAT LEAD INTO THIS JOB:

- Marketing Coordinator
- News Writer

KEY RESPONSIBILITIES:

- Developing strategies that support your company's image online
- Distributing press releases and pitching stories to journalists
- Working with press at live events to help provide great coverage

KEY REQUIREMENTS:

- Bachelor's degree in journalism or public relations
- Connections with journalists and other industry figures
- Past experience in a writing-based field

Don't like this job?
Try page 64

Like this job?
Try page 120

Requires a college degree

JOURNALISM & WRITING

EDITOR

As an Editor, you'll be responsible for overseeing the editorial work of your publication or company. This involves everything from copyediting to fact-checking for accuracy. You will guide staff and freelance writers on which topics to cover to ensure they meet your outlet's content plan — something you might help create. Due to this job's supervisory nature, it's suited for writers who already have a considerable amount of journalism experience and are comfortable having the final say on whether a story is ready for publication or not.

EXPERIENCE LEVEL:

Entry | Junior | Inter. | Senior

ROLES THIS JOB COULD UNLOCK:

- Head of Content
- Managing Editor

ROLES THAT LEAD INTO THIS JOB:

- Senior Writer
- Staff Writer

ADDITIONAL RESOURCE:

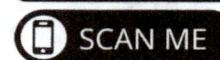 SCAN ME

KEY RESPONSIBILITIES:

- Defining your editorial guidelines, ethics and approach to reporting
- Editing work for spelling, grammar, accuracy and relevancy
- Mentoring writing staff to support their career development

KEY REQUIREMENTS:

- 2+ years as a professional writer
- Capable of mentoring junior writers in all aspects of journalism
- In-depth knowledge of esports, gaming and AP styling

Don't like this job?
Try page 49

Like this job?
Try page 78

Requires a college degree

JOURNALISM & WRITING

TOURNAMENT OPERATIONS

I got to play in an esports tournament once and loved it! I know there are lots of jobs on the team side of esports, but I'm more interested in learning about how the tournaments are built. Can I turn that into a job?

Certainly! There's nothing quite like the atmosphere of a live event, and these are the lifeblood of esports. They take a lot of work to plan and execute, which is only possible with the help of talented professionals.

That's great! Being part of a crew putting together esports events would be amazing. I'm not sure what job I would like best, though. I just know I want to be involved.

Hey, that's still a good starting point. Let's see what jobs exist in this section and if any catch your interest…

CONTINUE TO JOBS 26-31

REFEREE

As a Referee, you'll be responsible for upholding the competitive integrity of a competition. Referees are present at all major esports tournaments and play a vital role. Cheating, technical issues and rule violations can be the difference-maker in a match, so there needs to be somebody in a position of authority that can handle these issues when they come up. This is a very niche job due to the limited number of companies that hire in the area. Jobs here tend to be offered on a contract basis, which means it's important to build relationships with tournament operators so you're in their pool of candidates when they come to hire.

EXPERIENCE LEVEL:

Entry   Junior   Inter.   Senior

ROLES THIS JOB COULD UNLOCK:

- Director of Competition
- Tournament Manager

ADDITIONAL RESOURCE:

SCAN ME

ROLES THAT LEAD INTO THIS JOB:

- League Administrator
- Observer

KEY RESPONSIBILITIES:

- Making rulings on technical pauses, server resets and rule violations
- Observing official matches to ensure rules are upheld
- Performing pre-game checks to identify issues before matches

KEY REQUIREMENTS:

- Confident decision-making in a high-pressure environment
- Experience refereeing amateur tournaments
- Expert knowledge of your game and its competitive ruleset

Don't like this job?
Try page 82

Like this job?
Try page 51

Does not require a college degree

TOURNAMENT OPERATIONS

4

TOURNAMENT ADMIN

As a Tournament Administrator, you'll be responsible for the competitive experience at your event. You'll be in charge of managing the competition bracket, coordinating with teams and working with production to ensure a smooth show. If there's an online portion or qualifier to your event, then you'll also be administering its execution. Since this role is unique to esports, any experience you can gain in the amateur or collegiate scene will help you out massively down the road.

EXPERIENCE LEVEL:

Entry   Junior   Inter.   Senior

ROLES THIS JOB COULD UNLOCK:

- Director of Competition
- Head of Events

ROLES THAT LEAD INTO THIS JOB:

- Observer
- Referee

ADDITIONAL RESOURCE:

 SCAN ME

KEY RESPONSIBILITIES:

- Coordinating event updates to the production team and talent
- Managing team check-ins and the overall tournament experience
- Working with event staff to uphold competitive integrity

KEY REQUIREMENTS:

- 1+ years managing esports brackets, rulesets and competitions
- Extensive knowledge of your game and its competitive ruleset
- Prior experience as a referee, online tournament moderator or player

**Don't like this job?
Try page 24**

**Like this job?
Try page 51**

May require a college degree

TOURNAMENT OPERATIONS

47

EVENT MARKETER

As an Event Marketer, you'll be responsible for attracting online and in-person viewers to your events. You'll do this by remarketing to people who've previously engaged with your events, along with creating campaigns to reach an entirely new audience. A marketing background is key for this role, though more senior positions will also require dedicated events marketing experience. It's important that you're creative, deeply tapped into the esports audience and able to craft storylines that will hook them.

EXPERIENCE LEVEL:

Entry   **Junior**   **Inter.**   Senior

ROLES THIS JOB COULD UNLOCK:

- Head of Events
- Senior Marketing Manager

ROLES THAT LEAD INTO THIS JOB:

- Event Coordinator
- Marketing Coordinator

ADDITIONAL RESOURCE:

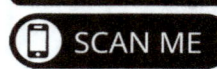

KEY RESPONSIBILITIES:

- Building marketing strategies to increase viewership and attendance
- Setting up remarketing campaigns and maintaining an email list
- Working with internal teams on creative activations

KEY REQUIREMENTS:

- 1+ years in marketing
- Endemic understanding of the esports community
- Past experience in events marketing or social media a plus

✕
Don't like this job?
Try page 76

✓
Like this job?
Try page 29

🎓
May require a college degree

TOURNAMENT OPERATIONS

IT MANAGER

As an IT Manager, you'll be responsible for providing technical support at live esports events. This ranges from setting up an environment that players can compete in, to facilitating a seamless technical production with the broadcast team. As such, this job is suited for people who are extremely technically literate and can act as a voice of authority on hardware, network and software issues. After an event has concluded, you'll also be putting together a report on how to safeguard against any problems that came up for the future.

EXPERIENCE LEVEL:

Entry   Junior   Inter.   Senior

ROLES THIS JOB COULD UNLOCK:

- Head of IT
- Technical Director

ADDITIONAL RESOURCE:

 SCAN ME

ROLES THAT LEAD INTO THIS JOB:

- IT Administrator
- Network Engineer

KEY RESPONSIBILITIES:

- Coordinating an event's technical setup and security
- Documenting problems during the event and proposing solutions
- Maintaining a best-in-class knowledge of equipment and software

KEY REQUIREMENTS:

- 1+ years in IT support
- 1+ years in networking
- Knowledge of cyber security and computer hardware

Don't like this job? Try page 39

Like this job? Try page 65

May require a college degree

TOURNAMENT OPERATIONS

49

EVENT MANAGER

As an Event Manager, you'll be responsible for the logistics and set up of an esports event. This position requires a strong project management background, as you'll be working with a number of third parties to line up everything that an event needs. Collecting experience in live events—even if it's from outside the esports industry—will help qualify you for this job. A good event manager will be comfortable managing people, budgets and time-sensitive deadlines.

EXPERIENCE LEVEL:

Entry   Junior   **Inter.**   Senior

ROLES THIS JOB COULD UNLOCK:

- Head of Events
- Head of Logistics

ADDITIONAL RESOURCE:

 SCAN ME

ROLES THAT LEAD INTO THIS JOB:

- Event Coordinator
- Logistics Manager

KEY RESPONSIBILITIES:

- Booking contractors across security, catering and other essentials
- Helping distribute the event budget
- Providing on-the-ground assistance during the event

KEY REQUIREMENTS:

- 2+ years in live events
- Excellent project management, negotiation and people managemen[t]
- Level-headed under pressure and able to plan well in advance

Don't like this job?
Try page 129

Like this job?
Try page 70

May require a college degree

TOURNAMENT OPERATIONS

DIRECTOR OF COMPETITION

As a Director of Competition, you'll be responsible for the overall creation of esports tournaments. This includes working with game publishers, production crews and venues to create high-quality experiences for both fans and players. This is a leadership role that requires veteran knowledge of the esports industry and its competitive circuit, as many of the major event decisions will be up to you. Building a professional profile in live events and league operations will set you up with the skills needed for this position.

EXPERIENCE LEVEL:

Entry Junior Inter. **Senior**

ROLES THIS JOB COULD UNLOCK:

- Chief Operating Officer
- VP of Competition

ROLES THAT LEAD INTO THIS JOB:

- League Operations Manager
- Senior Event Manager

ADDITIONAL RESOURCE:

 SCAN ME

KEY RESPONSIBILITIES:

- Building relationships with teams and managing communication
- Designing competitive structures, brackets and rulesets
- Overseeing the creation and execution of esports tournaments

KEY REQUIREMENTS:

- 3+ years in a managerial role
- 2+ years in tournament operations
- Past experience designing esports competitions from scratch

Don't like this job?
Try page 30

Like this job?
Try page 17

May require a college degree

TOURNAMENT OPERATIONS

ON-AIR TALENT

I found esports after stumbling across some pro matches on Twitch. It's a lot of fun to watch and the casters do a great job building the hype! I think they have the coolest job ever and I'd love to figure out how to do it myself.

Totally agreed, the on-air talent can really make an event! There is something you should keep in mind, though: it's one of the harder fields in esports to enter, but not impossible! It just takes a desire to improve and succeed.

Well, I am certain I want to at least give it a shot! How do I go about landing my first gig?

Landing your first on-air gig is certainly tricky, but let's work together to learn about the different jobs that exist here and what skills they require…

CONTINUE TO JOBS 32-35

PLAY-BY-PLAY CASTER

As a Play-by-Play Caster, you'll be responsible for covering the action of live esports matches. This is an on-camera role that requires advanced game knowledge and great spoken ability. Top play-by-play casters will be enthusiastic, engaging and able to provide commentary that helps viewers follow the game. Casters typically start their career on their own Twitch channels or at small, amateur events before working their way up the industry ladder. A video showreel is essential when applying to jobs in this area, even if you have to put it together by recording yourself casting over demo games!

EXPERIENCE LEVEL:

Entry   Junior   Inter.   Senior

ROLES THIS JOB COULD UNLOCK:

- Desk Analyst
- Head of Talent

ADDITIONAL RESOURCE:

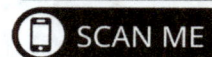 SCAN ME

ROLES THAT LEAD INTO THIS JOB:

- Content Creator
- Video Presenter/Interviewer

KEY RESPONSIBILITIES:

- Articulating fast-paced gameplay for viewers
- Breaking down strategies together with your color caster
- Maintaining a high level of energy throughout each broadcast

KEY REQUIREMENTS:

- A showreel of on-camera work (including self-recorded clips)
- Engaging, likable camera presence with advanced game knowledge
- Experience casting amateur or semi-professional tournaments

Don't like this job?
Try page 87

Like this job?
Try page 57

Does not require a college degree

ON-AIR TALENT

COLOR CASTER

As a Color Caster, you'll be responsible for providing strategy insights during live esports matches. This is an on-camera role that requires expert game knowledge and great research skills. Your job is to support your play-by-play partner's commentary with analysis of each team's strategy. As such, color casters need an even higher level of game knowledge than their play-by-play counterparts. Casters typically start their career on their own Twitch channels or at small, amateur events before working their way up the industry ladder. A video showreel is essential when applying to jobs in this area, even if you have to put it together by recording yourself casting over demo games!

EXPERIENCE LEVEL:

Entry   Junior   Inter.   Senior

ROLES THIS JOB COULD UNLOCK:

- Desk Analyst
- Head of Talent

ADDITIONAL RESOURCE:

SCAN ME

ROLES THAT LEAD INTO THIS JOB:

- Content Creator
- Professional Player

KEY RESPONSIBILITIES:

- Analyzing key plays and decisions throughout the match
- Maintaining a high level of energy throughout each broadcast
- Preparing notes on each team to add depth to your commentary

KEY REQUIREMENTS:

- A showreel of on-camera work (including self-recorded clips)
- Engaging, likable camera presence with expert game knowledge
- Experience casting amateur or semi-professional tournaments

Don't like this job?
Try page 23

Like this job?
Try page 57

Does not require a college degree

ON-AIR TALENT

DESK ANALYST

As a Desk Analyst, you'll be responsible for providing analysis in between live esports matches. This is an on-camera role that requires you to work with the desk host to break down the game that's just been played and set the stage for the one to come. The audience will look to you for an explanation of a game's key moments, so your game knowledge must be immaculate. A polished camera presence is important, too, so any experience you can gain at the amateur level of esports or in your own time will help in the long run.

EXPERIENCE LEVEL:

Entry   Junior   Inter.   Senior

ROLES THIS JOB COULD UNLOCK:

- Color Caster
- Head of Talent

ROLES THAT LEAD INTO THIS JOB:

- Professional Player
- Team Analyst

ADDITIONAL RESOURCE:

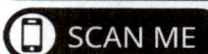 SCAN ME

KEY RESPONSIBILITIES:

- Dissecting high-level strategies in a way viewers can understand
- Highlighting what viewers should be paying attention to
- Maintaining a high level of energy throughout each broadcast

KEY REQUIREMENTS:

- A showreel of on-camera work (including self-recorded clips)
- Flawless game knowledge
- Prior experience as a professional player or team analyst a plus

Don't like this job?
Try page 116

Like this job?
Try page 12

Does not require a college degree

ON-AIR TALENT

DESK HOST

As a Desk Host, you'll be responsible for leading the desk segments during live esports tournaments. Alongside your desk analysts, you'll deconstruct the match that's just been played and build up storylines for the one to come. A producer or broadcast director will help guide you whenever there are delays in between matches, but you'll need to be a smooth conversationalist to keep the idle time between games interesting. Working in online leagues, conducting player interviews or even producing your own video content can all hone the skills needed in this role.

EXPERIENCE LEVEL:

Entry   Junior   Inter.   Senior

ROLES THIS JOB COULD UNLOCK:

- Head of Talent
- Producer

ROLES THAT LEAD INTO THIS JOB:

- Color Caster
- Play-by-Play Caster

ADDITIONAL RESOURCE:

 SCAN ME

KEY RESPONSIBILITIES:

- Carrying engaging conversations with your fellow on-air talent
- Promoting tournament sponsors
- Working with producers to keep the broadcast moving as intended

KEY REQUIREMENTS:

- A showreel of on-camera work (including self-recorded clips)
- Engaging, likable camera presence with good game knowledge
- Quick thinker with experience leading group conversations

**Don't like this job?
Try page 121**

**Like this job?
Try page 25**

Does not require a college degree

ON-AIR TALENT

BROADCASTING

I don't know if I want to be in front of a camera, but I'd still love to be a part of live events. I've messed around with streaming before and have OBS on my computer, but I'm guessing real broadcasts take more than that?

Streaming from home is a good way to learn the basics of broadcasting but yes, it does get more complicated at the professional level. For every major esports event you see on Twitch, there could be anywhere from 10 to 50 people working on the broadcasting team alone.

Wow, I had no idea it took that many people! Can you tell me what everyone does? Maybe then I can figure out which job is right for me.

Absolutely! Most broadcasting teams actually have multiple people in each of these roles. That means there are lots of opportunities to get started and work your way up. Let's have a more detailed look…

CONTINUE TO JOBS 36-42

IN-GAME OBSERVER

As an In-Game Observer, you'll be responsible for operating the in-game camera during a live esports match. It's a job that's unique to our industry, where you'll need expert control over your game's spectator mode so you can capture the best viewing experience possible. With each player's point-of-view available to you at any given time, it'll be your job to decide where the action is likely to take place and focus the in-game camera on this area. A good observer will have strong game sense in order to highlight as much action for the viewers as possible.

EXPERIENCE LEVEL:

Entry | Junior | Inter. | Senior

ROLES THIS JOB COULD UNLOCK:

- Line Producer
- Replay Operator

ADDITIONAL RESOURCE:

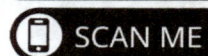
SCAN ME

ROLES THAT LEAD INTO THIS JOB:

- Amateur In-Game Observer
- Amateur Producer

KEY RESPONSIBILITIES:

- Capturing key moments on the in-game camera
- Maintaining a strong game and map knowledge in your title
- Telling a story through where the broadcast's focus is

KEY REQUIREMENTS:

- Complete knowledge of your game's spectator mode
- Prior experience in amateur or semi-professional observing a plus
- Strong instinct for which player to spectate at any given time

**Don't like this job?
Try page 106**

**Like this job?
Try page 26**

May require a college degree

BROADCASTING

REPLAY OPERATOR

As a Replay Operator, you'll be responsible for capturing the replay footage you see in esports broadcasts. You'll typically work in a broadcasting studio using either Parsec or vMix to capture and clip content. Due to the nature of this role, it's typically hired for on a contract or freelance basis, and could be totally remote if you're working on an online broadcast. The clearest route to entry is by familiarizing yourself with a broadcasting software like vMix and making use of this in the amateur or semi-pro scene.

EXPERIENCE LEVEL:

Entry Junior Inter. Senior

ROLES THIS JOB COULD UNLOCK:

- Line Producer
- Technical Director

ADDITIONAL RESOURCE:

SCAN ME

ROLES THAT LEAD INTO THIS JOB:

- Broadcasting Intern
- Observer

KEY RESPONSIBILITIES:

- Clipping gameplay footage during live esports matches
- Communicating with showrunners to clip content that fits their vision
- Seeking out replay opportunities wherever possible

KEY REQUIREMENTS:

- Expertise in Parsec, vMix or similar
- Familiarity with live broadcasts and their structure
- Prior experience in observing or live streaming a plus

Don't like this job? Try page 14

Like this job? Try page 66

May require a college degree

BROADCASTING

ON-AIR TALENT MANAGER

As an On-Air Talent Manager, you'll be responsible for supporting an event's casters, hosts and analysts. This could be through managing their schedules on rehearsal and broadcast days, to providing feedback when necessary. For this reason, having a background in broadcasting yourself is often a requirement. On-air talent managers also play a large role in the selection of on-air talent for each event, along with negotiating their day rates and the other details of their contract.

EXPERIENCE LEVEL:

Entry Junior Inter. Senior

ROLES THIS JOB COULD UNLOCK:
- Head of Talent
- Line Producer

ADDITIONAL RESOURCE:

 SCAN ME

ROLES THAT LEAD INTO THIS JOB:
- Any On-Air Talent Role
- Influencer Manager

KEY RESPONSIBILITIES:
- Booking talent for events and negotiating contracts
- Managing schedules and ensuring everyone is ready for broadcast
- Serving as the talent's point of contact during and after the event

KEY REQUIREMENTS:
- 2+ years working on-air in esports, sports or entertainment
- 1+ years managing creators, players or talent
- Experience with branding and marketing a plus

Don't like this job?
Try page 39

Like this job?
Try page 121

May require a college degree

BROADCASTING

GRAPHICS PRODUCER

As a Graphics Producer, you'll be responsible for the visual assets employed during a broadcast. Throughout an event you'll see numerous overlays, motion graphics, sponsor animations and transitions used, which is where this role comes in. Not only will you help design these assets, you'll also be loading them into your live streaming software for a line producer to access throughout the broadcast. So while graphic design experience is important, the candidates who are best suited for this position will be able to combine that with broadcasting knowledge.

EXPERIENCE LEVEL:

Entry   **Junior**   **Inter.**   Senior

ROLES THIS JOB COULD UNLOCK:

- Broadcast Director
- Line Producer

ADDITIONAL RESOURCE:

 SCAN ME

ROLES THAT LEAD INTO THIS JOB:

- Graphic Designer
- Production Assistant

KEY RESPONSIBILITIES:

- Designing key graphics to enhance the viewing experience
- Loading graphic packs into production software before each event
- Working with line producers to queue graphics during a broadcast

KEY REQUIREMENTS:

- 1+ years on a broadcasting team
- 1+ years of graphic design experience
- A varied design portfolio featuring static and motion graphics

**Don't like this job?
Try page 105**

**Like this job?
Try page 34**

**May require a
college degree**

BROADCASTING

LINE PRODUCER

As a Line Producer, you'll be responsible for managing the run-of-show during a broadcast. A run-of-show is a detailed schedule of what the stream will include, such as content segments and desk analysis. Your job is to follow this as closely as possible to avoid delays, while also having material prepared for if there are any unexpected stoppages during an event. Line producers will lead rehearsals ahead of a broadcast and are constantly communicating with on-air talent to advise them when to hurry through a segment, prolong it or make any other adjustments.

EXPERIENCE LEVEL:

Entry   Junior   **Inter.**   Senior

ROLES THIS JOB COULD UNLOCK:

- Broadcast Director
- Head of Production

ROLES THAT LEAD INTO THIS JOB:

- Production Assistant
- Replay Operator

KEY RESPONSIBILITIES:

- Adjusting show timings to account for delays
- Managing the run-of-show during a broadcast
- Preparing content segments and other materials for broadcast

KEY REQUIREMENTS:

- 2+ years of live broadcast experience
- 1+ years in a production environment
- Prior experience building run-of-shows a plus

ADDITIONAL RESOURCE:

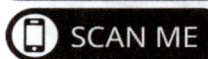 SCAN ME

 Don't like this job?
Try page 47

 Like this job?
Try page 66

 May require a college degree

 **BROADCASTING**

TECHNICAL DIRECTOR

As a Technical Director, you'll be responsible for the audio-visual (A/V), lighting and technology used during a broadcast. This means ensuring your company has all of the tools needed to produce a professional live show or outsourcing elements of it to a third-party. As a supervisory position, you'll need to be a subject expert in broadcast technology and comfortable managing people. You'll need a significant amount of experience to qualify, and while it helps to have this in esports, it's usually accepted for people to transition from sports, entertainment or a similar industry as well.

EXPERIENCE LEVEL:

Entry   Junior   Inter.   **Senior**

ROLES THIS JOB COULD UNLOCK:
- Broadcast Director
- Head of Technology

ADDITIONAL RESOURCE:

 SCAN ME

ROLES THAT LEAD INTO THIS JOB:
- A/V Technician
- Technical Manager

KEY RESPONSIBILITIES:
- Managing the technical infrastructure needed to produce a live event
- Resolving tech problems during an event as swiftly as possible
- Setting up A/V, lighting and production tools ahead of events

KEY REQUIREMENTS:
- 5+ years on a broadcasting team
- 2+ years in a management position
- Capable of setting up a live event's technology from scratch

 Don't like this job? Try page 12

 Like this job? Try page 49

 May require a college degree

 BROADCASTING

BROADCAST DIRECTOR

As a Broadcast Director, you'll be responsible for overseeing the production of a live broadcast. You'll work with your line producers, on-air talent and all other departments to deliver the best viewership experience possible. This is a broad, supervisory position where you'll shape the run-of-show, highlight event storylines and hand-select each shot that makes it into the broadcast. People management is an equally important part of this job. Due to the nature of working in live events, you'll need to be comfortable making decisions in a fast and confident manner, while keeping your team motivated and focused towards your vision.

EXPERIENCE LEVEL:

Entry   Junior   Inter.   Senior

ROLES THIS JOB COULD UNLOCK:

- Creative Director
- Head of Events

ROLES THAT LEAD INTO THIS JOB:

- Line Producer
- Technical Director

ADDITIONAL RESOURCE:

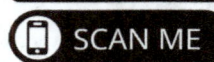 SCAN ME

KEY RESPONSIBILITIES:

- Choosing which camera or video feed to display during live events
- Managing the broadcast team & helping them grow as professionals
- Overseeing the run-of-show throughout the broadcast

KEY REQUIREMENTS:

- 5+ years on a broadcasting team
- 2+ years managing people
- Confident decision-making and creative vision

Don't like this job? Try page 108

Like this job? Try page 51

May require a college degree

BROADCAST

CONTINUE TO GAME
PUBLISHERS

GAME PUBLISHERS

It seems like most games with an esports scene are made by the same few studios. I'm curious how these companies fit into the industry. Do they have jobs on the esports side of things or do they only hire game devs?

That's actually a great question. Esports started as groups of friends getting together to compete in their favorite video games. We've come a long way since then and most titles with an active esports community now receive direct support from their publishers.

I'm sure it would be fun to work with a publisher and see exactly how they operate. What kind of jobs are available there?

Well, we could write a whole other book about the jobs involved at a game studio, but for today let's focus on the esports department and some of the roles needed to support a competitive scene…

CONTINUE TO JOBS 43-46

PROJECT MANAGER

As a Project Manager, you'll be responsible for managing your studio's activities in esports. Depending on how hands-on your company is with its competitive scene, this could range from choosing locations, venues and schedules for its tournaments, to coordinating in-game activations like unique collectibles. It's a varied role that will differ from company to company, but will typically require a strong sense for business along with expert esports knowledge. As such, these jobs require candidates with direct experience in the industry.

EXPERIENCE LEVEL:

Entry   Junior   Inter.   Senior

ROLES THIS JOB COULD UNLOCK:

- Esports Director
- Esports Operations Manager

ADDITIONAL RESOURCE:

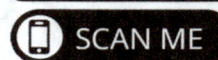 SCAN ME

ROLES THAT LEAD INTO THIS JOB:

- Account Manager
- Project Coordinator

KEY RESPONSIBILITIES:

- Acting as your game's ambassador within the esports community
- Developing projects that support your publisher's esports scene
- Working on official leagues or tournaments your publisher operates

KEY REQUIREMENTS:

- 2+ years in esports professionally
- Experience coordinating projects from start to finish
- In-depth knowledge of the esports ecosystem a necessity

Don't like this job?
Try page 54

Like this job?
Try page 116

May require a college degree

GAME PUBLISHERS

PARTNERSHIPS MANAGER

As a Partnerships Manager, you'll be responsible for sourcing, managing and negotiating partnership agreements for your studio. This job has similarities to a licensing manager, except you will primarily be working to develop partnerships outside of IP rights. These could drive brand awareness for your game's esports scene, revenue growth or a combination of both. It's your job to fully understand the goals of your company within esports and seek out partnerships that support those.

EXPERIENCE LEVEL:

Entry   **Junior**   **Inter.**   Senior

ROLES THIS JOB COULD UNLOCK:

- Esports Director
- Head of Partnerships

ADDITIONAL RESOURCE:

 SCAN ME

ROLES THAT LEAD INTO THIS JOB:

- Account Manager
- Business Development Associate

KEY RESPONSIBILITIES:

- Managing the partnership submission process for your company
- Monitoring and reporting on existing partnerships
- Negotiating partnership agreements

KEY REQUIREMENTS:

- 2+ years in esports professionally
- 1+ years negotiating and managing partnerships
- Effective reporting and data analysis skills

Don't like this job? Try page 128

Like this job? Try page 86

May require a college degree

GAME PUBLISHERS

BRAND MANAGER

As a Brand Manager, you'll be responsible for defining how your studio and its esports scene are presented online. This could include working with partners and tournament organizers to ensure the game is being portrayed accurately, or defining your own online voice if your studio manages its esports initiatives directly. You will also track your studio's reputation online through techniques like social listening and produce reports for your team. This job requires a mix of marketing, social media and esports experience.

EXPERIENCE LEVEL:

Entry   Junior   Inter.   Senior

ROLES THIS JOB COULD UNLOCK:

- Head of Brand
- Marketing Director

ADDITIONAL RESOURCE:

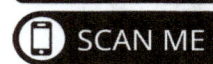 SCAN ME

ROLES THAT LEAD INTO THIS JOB:

- Brand Coordinator
- Marketing Assistant

KEY RESPONSIBILITIES:

- Defining your brand's voice, target audience and overall message
- Tracking online sentiment and making suggestions to improve it
- Working with internal teams to ensure they understand your vision

KEY REQUIREMENTS:

- 2+ years in marketing
- 1+ years in esports professionally
- Excellent written and verbal communication skills

Don't like this job?
Try page 41

Like this job?
Try page 77

May require a college degree

GAME PUBLISHERS

LICENSING MANAGER

As a Licensing Manager, you'll be responsible for sourcing, managing and negotiating licensing deals for your studio. You'll typically focus on a single game title, but might represent multiple in senior roles or at companies with a wide portfolio. Since your company owns the intellectual property (IP) to its game, it'll be your job to work with third parties interested in using it as an esports title. This includes vetting potential partners and negotiating deals on your company's behalf. Ultimately, you'll ensure your IP is being represented accurately and in a way that benefits your business.

EXPERIENCE LEVEL:

Entry   Junior   Inter.   Senior

ROLES THIS JOB COULD UNLOCK:

- Director of Business Development
- Director of Licensing

ADDITIONAL RESOURCE:

 SCAN ME

ROLES THAT LEAD INTO THIS JOB:

- Business Development Manager
- Licensing Coordinator

KEY RESPONSIBILITIES:

- Developing a licensing strategy for your company's esports division
- Evaluating partnership requests and seeking revenue opportunities
- Managing relationships with organizers, pro teams and other partners

KEY REQUIREMENTS:

- 2+ years in licensing and business development
- Excellent negotiation skills
- In-depth understanding of how different businesses operate

Don't like this job? Try page 107

Like this job? Try page 98

May require a college degree

GAME PUBLISHERS

COLLEGIATE ESPORTS

I heard that students are now going to college for esports and can even get scholarships for it! Is that true? It would be amazing for esports to be viewed the same as traditional sports in school.

That's right! Colleges and universities all over the world are beginning to develop esports degree programs, with some even offering full-ride scholarships to promising players. The first college esports program was started in 2014, and since then hundreds more have followed suit.

Wow, esports really is everywhere! Does that mean college esports programs have their own coaches and staff like a professional team would?

That's correct! A lot of these college esports programs are structured like mini professional teams. They hire coaches to work with the players and have their own esports labs to practice in! Let's take a look at some of the jobs that make up the collegiate esports scene…

CONTINUE TO JOBS 47-50

COLLEGIATE COACH

As a Collegiate Coach, you'll be in charge of a competitive esports team at your university or college. This role hhas significant overlap with a traditional coach's responsibilities, including leading practices, setting up scrims and helping players improve their game. You'll need in-game knowledge for your chosen title to qualify for this role, and any amateur or semi-professional coaching experience will be a major plus. An eye for talent is important, too, as you'll spend a large amount of your time scouting new players to bring into your program.

EXPERIENCE LEVEL:

Entry | Junior | Inter. | Senior

ROLES THIS JOB COULD UNLOCK:

- Amateur/Professional Coach
- Program Director

ADDITIONAL RESOURCE:

 SCAN ME

ROLES THAT LEAD INTO THIS JOB:

- Amateur Coach
- Amateur/Collegiate Player

KEY RESPONSIBILITIES:

- Establishing a practice schedule and leading each session
- Recruiting new students to your program through smart outreach
- Working with individual players to identify where they can improve

KEY REQUIREMENTS:

- 1+ years in esports experience
- Expert game knowledge essential; prior competitive experience a plus
- Highly organized with strong program management skills

Don't like this job?
Try page 50

Like this job?
Try page 16

Requires a college degree

COLLEGIATE ESPORTS

COLLEGIATE LEAD

As a Collegiate Lead, you'll be responsible for representing a brand's presence in collegiate esports. Companies that hire for this role include hardware/peripheral brands, esports organizations and other industry service providers. This is the only job in this section not employed by an educational institution. Depending on your company's goals, you will establish partnerships that either drive brand awareness for your products among students, or help you build a pipeline of student athletes that might later compete in your organization. While doing this, you'll also be directly supporting the collegiate scene.

EXPERIENCE LEVEL:

Entry Junior Inter. Senior

ROLES THIS JOB COULD UNLOCK:

- Marketing Lead
- Program Director

ROLES THAT LEAD INTO THIS JOB:

- Marketing Manager
- Project Manager

ADDITIONAL RESOURCE:

SCAN ME

KEY RESPONSIBILITIES:

- Building partnerships in the collegiate esports scene
- Cementing your brand's presence in the collegiate esports scene
- Leading student-driven programs that build positive sentiment

KEY REQUIREMENTS:

- 2+ years in esports professionally
- 1+ years in marketing, sponsorship or project management
- Creative thinker who is able to build brand loyalty in young people

Don't like this job?
Try page 28

Like this job?
Try page 90

Requires a college degree

COLLEGIATE ESPORTS

ESPORTS LECTURER

As an Esports Lecturer, you'll be responsible for structuring an esports curriculum and delivering it to students. You will work alongside your dean or department head to identify suitable modules to include. Esports is still a new addition in college, which means you'll need to be comfortable working without reference material and building much of the curriculum yourself. Endemic industry knowledge, then, is vital, as is the ability to present your ideas clearly. Ultimately, your goal is to equip students with the skills they need to land a job in esports after graduating.

EXPERIENCE LEVEL:

Entry   Junior   **Inter.**   Senior

ROLES THIS JOB COULD UNLOCK:

- Program Director
- Senior Lecturer

ADDITIONAL RESOURCE:

 SCAN ME

ROLES THAT LEAD INTO THIS JOB:

- Any Full Time Esports Job
- Collegiate Coach

KEY RESPONSIBILITIES:

- Developing an educational curriculum around esports
- Presenting your curriculum to students through lectures
- Supporting individual students with areas they're struggling in

KEY REQUIREMENTS:

- 2+ years in esports professionally
- Ph.D, Master's or Bachelor's degree in any topic
- Top communication skills, especially to teenagers and young adults

Don't like this job? Try page 116

Like this job? Try page 79

Requires a college degree

COLLEGIATE ESPORTS

PROGRAM DIRECTOR

As a Program Director, you'll be responsible for the entire esports department at your college or university. You will work with your coaching staff to build the best competitive teams possible. A key success metric in this role is how many students are enrolling in the esports program, which all comes from setting up a valuable experience for your each and every member. Since this job is employed by an educational institute, a degree is nearly always required, though it often doesn't matter in what specialism.

EXPERIENCE LEVEL:

Entry   Junior   Inter.   Senior

ROLES THIS JOB COULD UNLOCK:

- Head of Operations
- Head of Program Management

ADDITIONAL RESOURCE:

 SCAN ME

ROLES THAT LEAD INTO THIS JOB:

- Collegiate Coach
- Esports Lecturer

KEY RESPONSIBILITIES:

- Developing esports guidelines to provide a great student experience
- Managing the esports budget, scholarship offers and recruitment
- Working directly with coaching staff to optimize each esports team

KEY REQUIREMENTS:

- 2+ years in education professionally
- 2+ years in esports professionally
- Senior-level program management and people management skills

Don't like this job? Try page 61

Like this job? Try page 17

Requires a college degree

COLLEGIATE ESPORTS

BUSINESS OPERATIONS

When I think of esports, I think about players and competition, but I'm starting to realize that's only one part of the industry. There's more opportunities beyond that than I ever realized.

That's right, while esports has a number of jobs that are unique to our industry, there are also countless back-office roles that are essential to powering the companies that move esports forward.

That makes a lot of sense. There have to be people that operate the businesses, too. Can we talk about some of those opportunities?

Certainly! Remember, these jobs exist in nearly every single industry, so you can actually build your early experience outside of esports and use that to work your way in. Let's take a look at some of your options…

CONTINUE TO JOBS 51-67

CUSTOMER SERVICE REP

As a Customer Service Representative, you'll be responsible for resolving customer issues. Whether it's over email, live chat, phone or in-person, you'll work to understand the problem that a customer is facing and advise them on the best solution. This is often an entry level or junior position and can be a great starting point for building a career in esports. It requires basic customer service skills and clear communication. That's usually it! From here, you could look to transition into sales or business development, or progress to the senior levels of customer support.

EXPERIENCE LEVEL:

Entry | Junior | Inter. | Senior

ROLES THIS JOB COULD UNLOCK:

- Junior Account Manager
- Sales Associate

ADDITIONAL RESOURCE:

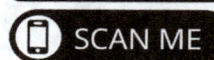 SCAN ME

ROLES THAT LEAD INTO THIS JOB:

- Hospitality Staff
- Retail Sales Assistant

KEY RESPONSIBILITIES:

- Addressing customer concerns and providing quick solutions
- Referring customers to other departments when required
- Representing your company in a professional and friendly manner

KEY REQUIREMENTS:

- Comfortable resolving problems over the phone, email or in-person
- Friendly and approachable personality
- In-depth knowledge of your company's services or products

Don't like this job?
Try page 25

Like this job?
Try page 86

Does not require a college degree

BUSINESS OPERATIONS

SALES ASSOCIATE

As a Sales Associate, you'll be responsible for building a pipeline of potential clients for your company. You'll use a CRM (customer relationship management) software to input client details, log what communication your company has had with them and file monthly activity reports. You may also lead the introductory meeting between your company and a potential client, so interpersonal skills are a must. This job is a great starting point to build a career in business.

EXPERIENCE LEVEL:

Entry Junior Inter. Senior

ROLES THIS JOB COULD UNLOCK:

- Account Manager
- Business Development Manager

ADDITIONAL RESOURCE:

 SCAN ME

ROLES THAT LEAD INTO THIS JOB:

- Retail Sales Assistant
- Sales Intern

KEY RESPONSIBILITIES:

- Building a pipeline of potential clients in a CRM
- Maintaining a thorough understanding of what your company offers
- Setting up introductory meetings with potential clients

KEY REQUIREMENTS:

- 6+ months in retail sales or customer service
- Basic customer service skills
- Self-motivated and driven personality

Don't like this job?
Try page 120

Like this job?
Try page 92

May require a college degree

BUSINESS OPERATIONS

OFFICE MANAGER

As an Office Manager, you'll be responsible for maintaining your company's office. You'll work on reception to greet visitors, take deliveries and ensure the office is running efficiently. Some of your other tasks will include directing messages to the correct department, arranging corporate events and managing the office's inventory of snacks, drinks and equipment. This is an administrative position that doesn't require a background in esports, making it possible to transition into after building experience in another industry.

EXPERIENCE LEVEL:

Entry   Junior   Inter.   Senior

ROLES THIS JOB COULD UNLOCK:

- Executive Assistant
- HR Manager

ADDITIONAL RESOURCE:

 SCAN ME

ROLES THAT LEAD INTO THIS JOB:

- Administrative Assistant
- HR Coordinator

KEY RESPONSIBILITIES:

- Handling admin tasks such as booking travel and drafting documents
- Running a productive office by keeping it well-equipped & presented
- Supporting company culture by planning events and celebrations

KEY REQUIREMENTS:

- 1+ years in administration
- Highly organized, reliable and dependable
- Hospitality and customer service skills

Don't like this job?
Try page 39

Like this job?
Try page 128

May require a college degree

BUSINESS OPERATIONS

ACCOUNTANT

As an Accountant, you'll be responsible for the bookkeeping and financial reporting of your company. You will work under a chief financial officer on profit and loss statements , balance sheets, budgets and tax returns. Depending on the size of your employer, you may also be tasked with coordinating the monthly payroll and assisting with financial planning. This is a role with a clear route of entry: companies will be looking for candidates with a bachelor's degree in accounting and a certified public accountant (CPA) license.

EXPERIENCE LEVEL:

Entry **Junior** **Inter.** **Senior**

ROLES THIS JOB COULD UNLOCK:

- Head of Finance
- Tax Manager

ADDITIONAL RESOURCE:

 SCAN ME

ROLES THAT LEAD INTO THIS JOB:

- Accounting Intern
- Junior Accountant

KEY RESPONSIBILITIES:

- Ensuring monthly payroll is accurate and on-time each month
- Managing all bookkeeping, expenses and budgeting tasks
- Preparing financial statements and official returns

KEY REQUIREMENTS:

- Bachelor's degree in accounting or similar
- CPA license or the equivalent in your country of residence
- Exceptional math skills and attention to detail

Don't like this job?
Try page 117

Like this job?
Try page 91

Requires a college degree

BUSINESS OPERATIONS

85

ACCOUNT MANAGER

As an Account Manager, you'll be responsible for securing new corporate clients for your company and maintaining existing ones. This is a business development position with an emphasis on customer satisfaction. You will manage a portfolio of clients to ensure their needs are met and, crucially, that they remain customers in the future. You'll also support your company's product by passing on feedback from its most active users. This is typically a junior position that requires sales and customer service experience, so it can be an effective way to get your foot in the door of esports.

EXPERIENCE LEVEL:

Entry | Junior | Inter. | Senior

ROLES THIS JOB COULD UNLOCK:

- Account Director
- Business Development Manager

ADDITIONAL RESOURCE:

 SCAN ME

ROLES THAT LEAD INTO THIS JOB:

- Customer Experience Coordinator
- Sales Associate

KEY RESPONSIBILITIES:

- Listening to feedback from clients and passing it to your developers
- Maintaining a positive client relationship through regular check-ins
- Networking with potential clients and understanding their needs

KEY REQUIREMENTS:

- 1+ years in sales or business development
- Ability to understand a digital product fully and explain its benefits
- Excellent customer service skills

Don't like this job? Try page 23

Like this job? Try page 116

May require a college degree

BUSINESS OPERATIONS

RESEARCH ANALYST

As a Research Analyst, you'll be responsible for building insights for your company or on behalf of a client. The focus of this research will depend on your employer: you might be analyzing new markets to expand into, researching possible acquisition targets or building data reports for a research firm. A common research framework is the SWOT analysis, which stands for 'strengths, weaknesses, opportunities and threats'. Meticulous, data-driven people thrive in this role, so employers will be looking for backgrounds in market research, data analysis or statistics.

EXPERIENCE LEVEL:

Entry Junior Inter. Senior

ROLES THIS JOB COULD UNLOCK:

- Business Intelligence Manager
- Head of Research

ADDITIONAL RESOURCE:

 SCAN ME

ROLES THAT LEAD INTO THIS JOB:

- Junior Data Analyst
- Research Assistant

KEY RESPONSIBILITIES:

- Conducting market research on companies, regions and trends
- Performing a SWOT analysis to highlight your takeaways
- Visualizing data you collect so it can be easily viewed by colleagues

KEY REQUIREMENTS:

- 1+ years in market research or data analysis
- Able to visualize data clearly and provide insights from it
- Expertise in Excel or a similar data processing tool

Don't like this job?
Try page 50

Like this job?
Try page 105

Requires a college degree

BUSINESS OPERATIONS

DATA ANALYST

As a Data Analyst, you'll be responsible for drawing actionable insights from business data. You'll work in a programming language called SQL to analyze large data sets and drive smart decision-making across the organization. Data insights can help teams understand which marketing campaigns perform best, how their website or app is used and what drives people to make purchases. This role suits people with a background in programming, statistics or data visualization, and esports experience is not usually required here.

EXPERIENCE LEVEL:

Entry   Junior   Inter.   Senior

ROLES THIS JOB COULD UNLOCK:

- Business Intelligence Manager
- Head of Data

ADDITIONAL RESOURCE:

 SCAN ME

ROLES THAT LEAD INTO THIS JOB:

- Junior Data Analyst
- Junior Researcher

KEY RESPONSIBILITIES:

- Defining the data points you'd like to track and setting these up
- Performing data analysis to assist different departments
- Turning your analysis into easy-to-digest graphs and visualizations

KEY REQUIREMENTS:

- 2+ years working with data and running queries
- Fluency in SQL; additional programming languages a plus
- Highly analytical personality

Don't like this job?
Try page 70

Like this job?
Try page 104

Requires a college degree

BUSINESS OPERATIONS

BIZ DEV MANAGER

As a Business Development Manager, you'll be responsible for driving revenue for your company through partnerships, sponsorships and other opportunities. This is typically quite a free-form job; while you may have some direction from your supervisors, you'll have a lot of freedom to decide which opportunities to pursue. Successful business developers will have an in-depth knowledge of the esports market, allowing them to spot opportunities where their company's services are required. If you can fuse creative thinking with detailed product knowledge and a skill for sales, then this could be a career path for you.

EXPERIENCE LEVEL:

Entry Junior **Inter.** Senior

ROLES THIS JOB COULD UNLOCK:

- Account Director
- Head of Sales

ADDITIONAL RESOURCE:

 SCAN ME

ROLES THAT LEAD INTO THIS JOB:

- Account Manager
- Sales Associate

KEY RESPONSIBILITIES:

- Conducting market research to identify new business opportunities
- Negotiating deals with partners to maximize revenue
- Pitching sponsorship deals to partners in a clear, effective way

KEY REQUIREMENTS:

- 2+ years in partnerships or sales
- Experience negotiating contract terms
- Highly-motivated personality

Don't like this job?
Try page 62

Like this job?
Try page 125

May require a college degree

BUSINESS OPERATIONS

ESPORTS LEAD

As an Esports Lead, you'll be responsible for managing a non-endemic brand's activity in the esports market. Non-endemic brands—like fast-food chains or car manufacturers—will often choose to advertise their products to the highly-desirable esports audience: tech-savvy young adults. In this role, you'll shape partnerships and activations that will establish your company's footprint in esports. An authentic understanding of the industry is essential to doing that, as is a track record of building sponsorship campaigns over several years.

EXPERIENCE LEVEL:

Entry   Junior   **Inter.**   **Senior**

ROLES THIS JOB COULD UNLOCK:

- Head of Marketing
- Head of Sponsorships

ADDITIONAL RESOURCE:

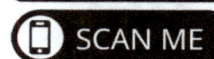 SCAN ME

ROLES THAT LEAD INTO THIS JOB:

- Account Manager
- Brand Manager

KEY RESPONSIBILITIES:

- Driving brand awareness through esports activations and events
- Inserting your brand into the esports conversation authentically
- Sourcing partnerships that compliment your business goals

KEY REQUIREMENTS:

- 3+ years in sponsorships or marketing
- 2+ years in esports professionally
- A track record of managing sponsorships yourself from start to finish

Don't like this job?
Try page 130

Like this job?
Try page 77

May require a college degree

BUSINESS OPERATIONS

FINANCIAL ANALYST

As a Financial Analyst, you'll be responsible for conducting financial research to help your company make smart business decisions. This job has similarities to an accountant, but is much more focused on business strategy. Working in either a specific department or the company as a whole, you'll produce analysis to help your colleagues understand the finances behind large projects. This is essential in large companies, as even small changes in pricing can make a colossal difference to their bottom line.

EXPERIENCE LEVEL:

Entry   Junior   Inter.   Senior

ROLES THIS JOB COULD UNLOCK:

- Head of Finance
- Senior Financial Analyst

ADDITIONAL RESOURCE:

 SCAN ME

ROLES THAT LEAD INTO THIS JOB:

- Accountant
- Data Analyst

KEY RESPONSIBILITIES:

- Developing projections around products, pricing changes and more
- Preparing regular financial performance reports
- Providing data your company needs to make wise business decisions

KEY REQUIREMENTS:

- 2+ years in finance or data analysis
- Bachelor's degree in finance
- Mastery of Excel, with the ability to use advanced formulas

Don't like this job? Try page 22

Like this job? Try page 95

Requires a college degree

BUSINESS OPERATIONS

HEAD OF SALES

As a Head of Sales, you'll be responsible for managing your company's sales department. This will usually include defining the sales strategy you'll use, instilling this in your colleagues and mentoring junior sales staff. Since this is a department lead position, you'll also need to be comfortable reporting your performance to senior leaders. To qualify for the role, you'll need to have built a stellar track record in sales and picked up some people management experience along the way.

EXPERIENCE LEVEL:

Entry Junior Inter. Senior

ROLES THIS JOB COULD UNLOCK:

- Chief Revenue Officer
- VP of Sales

ADDITIONAL RESOURCE:

 SCAN ME

ROLES THAT LEAD INTO THIS JOB:

- Account Manager
- Business Development Manager

KEY RESPONSIBILITIES:

- Managing the day-to-day operations of your sales team
- Mentoring junior staff to help them achieve their full potential
- Reporting sales figures on a monthly, quarterly and annual basis

KEY REQUIREMENTS:

- 5+ years in sales
- 2+ years managing direct reports
- Well-connected in the esports and entertainment industry

Don't like this job?
Try page 41

Like this job?
Try page 73

May require a college degree

BUSINESS OPERATIONS

INTERNAL COMMS MANAGER

As an Internal Communications Manager, you'll be responsible for managing the communications within a company. In large companies, when everybody has a specific focus, it can be difficult to know what's happening elsewhere in the organization. This can be especially problematic when two departments need to work together, like product and sales. Your job is to facilitate clear communication throughout the company through memos, updates and internal procedures. Therefore, you'll need to demonstrate professional experience in writing through experience in PR, marketing or a similar field.

EXPERIENCE LEVEL:

Entry   Junior   Inter.   Senior

ROLES THIS JOB COULD UNLOCK:
- Head of Communications
- PR Manager

ADDITIONAL RESOURCE:

 SCAN ME

ROLES THAT LEAD INTO THIS JOB:
- Content Writer
- PR Coordinator

KEY RESPONSIBILITIES:
- Determining the best tools to improve internal communication
- Meeting with employees to understand communication problems
- Preparing internal memos to keep staff members informed

KEY REQUIREMENTS:
- 1+ years in communications or public relations
- Knowledge of how different company departments work together
- Outstanding written ability

Don't like this job?
Try page 47

Like this job?
Try page 120

May require a college degree

BUSINESS OPERATIONS

PRODUCT MANAGER

As a Product Manager, you'll be responsible for the go-to-market strategy and execution of a new product offering. This could be a digital product, like a website or app, or a physical product like a new headset line. In the planning stage of this job, you'll be working with your development team to ensure the product is delivered on time and at a high quality. Then you'll manage its launch and regularly report on the performance of your product line. It's a varied role, and requires someone well-versed in business with experience managing projects, people and budgets.

EXPERIENCE LEVEL:

Entry | Junior | Inter. | Senior

ROLES THIS JOB COULD UNLOCK:

- Head of Product
- Product Lead

ROLES THAT LEAD INTO THIS JOB:

- Associate Product Manager
- Project Manager

ADDITIONAL RESOURCE:

SCAN ME

KEY RESPONSIBILITIES:

- Overseeing product development to keep it on time and on budget
- Setting a go-to-market plan and executing it
- Tracking key performance indicators for your product

KEY REQUIREMENTS:

- 2+ years in project management or product development
- 1+ years leading a team
- Comfortable with budget management, drafting reports & data analy

Don't like this job?
Try page 128

Like this job?
Try page 70

May require a college degree

BUSINESS OPERATIONS

FINANCE MANAGER

As a Finance Manager, you'll be responsible for a variety of financial tasks, typically at a small to mid-sized company. This is a generalist role, meaning if an esports organization or startup can't justify making multiple finance hires they'll look for a person like this. Responsibilities are likely to be a blend with accounting: handling bookkeeping while also supporting financial analysis. The requirements are largely the same, too: you'll need a degree in a relevant field and a CPA license (however, unlike accountancy jobs, this isn't always required).

EXPERIENCE LEVEL:

Entry   Junior   Inter.   Senior

ROLES THIS JOB COULD UNLOCK:
- CFO
- Head of Finance

ADDITIONAL RESOURCE:

SCAN ME

ROLES THAT LEAD INTO THIS JOB:
- Accountant
- Financial Analyst

KEY RESPONSIBILITIES:
- Managing a variety of finance tasks
- Monitoring accounts payable & receivable to ensure proper cash flow
- Performing financial analysis to support business decisions

KEY REQUIREMENTS:
- 3+ years in finance
- Bachelor's degree in finance
- Exceptional math skills and mastery of Excel

Don't like this job?
Try page 64

Like this job?
Try page 136

Requires a college degree

BUSINESS OPERATIONS

LEGAL COUNSEL

As Legal Counsel, you'll be responsible for guiding your company in all legal matters. This could range from drafting employment contracts to reviewing partnership agreements. When the company is launching new products or expanding into new territories, you'll need to make sure that they've complied with all local regulations. This is a role that's only available to qualified legal professionals; jobs in this area will always ask for a relevant degree and at least a couple of years spent practicing law. It won't usually ask for any type of background in esports.

EXPERIENCE LEVEL:

Entry   Junior   **Inter.**   **Senior**

ROLES THIS JOB COULD UNLOCK:

- Chief Legal Officer
- Senior Counsel

ROLES THAT LEAD INTO THIS JOB:

- Lawyer
- Legal Assistant

ADDITIONAL RESOURCE:

 SCAN ME

KEY RESPONSIBILITIES:

- Being the company's authority on legal matters
- Drafting and reviewing legal documents across the business
- Providing counsel on employment, fundraising and partnerships

KEY REQUIREMENTS:

- 2+ years as a practicing lawyer
- Bachelor's and Juris Doctor degree
- Capable of explaining complex legal matters in simpler terms

Don't like this job?
Try page 79

Like this job?
Try page 133

Requires a college degree

BUSINESS OPERATIONS

EXECUTIVE ASSISTANT

As an Executive Assistant, you'll be responsible for supporting a senior company executive in their day-to-day tasks. This includes managing their calendar, scheduling meetings and booking travel arrangements. You'll also attend meetings to record 'minutes' (written notes) and ensure all agenda items have been covered. Ultimately, your goal is to relieve some of the stress that comes with an executive position by handling their smaller tasks and serving, at least partly, as an advisor. This is a senior-level role that requires someone highly qualified in administration.

EXPERIENCE LEVEL:

Entry   Junior   Inter.   **Senior**

ROLES THIS JOB COULD UNLOCK:

- Chief of Staff
- Head of Administration

ADDITIONAL RESOURCE:

 SCAN ME

ROLES THAT LEAD INTO THIS JOB:

- Administrative Manager
- Office Manager

KEY RESPONSIBILITIES:

- Advising the executive on key decisions
- Maintaining confidentiality when dealing with sensitive topics
- Managing all administrative tasks for the executive

KEY REQUIREMENTS:

- 5+ years in administration
- Extremely high attention to detail, reliability and organization skills
- In-depth knowledge of the executive's department (marketing, HR, etc)

Don't like this job?
Try page 117

Like this job?
Try page 138

May require a college degree

BUSINESS OPERATIONS

COUNTRY MANAGER

As a Country Manager, you'll be responsible for coordinating your company's operations in a specific country or region. This is a senior-level role that's hired for by organizations expanding into a new market — like an esports team building a Brazilian division, for example. Together with your company's leadership, you'll define goals for this region, set a go-to-market plan and outline staffing needs that you have. Employers will be looking for senior business leaders in this role with experience in people management and, crucially, an understanding of the local market. It's a major plus if you're bilingual, too.

EXPERIENCE LEVEL:

Entry	Junior	Inter.	Senior

ROLES THIS JOB COULD UNLOCK:

- COO
- Head of Operations

ADDITIONAL RESOURCE:

 SCAN ME

ROLES THAT LEAD INTO THIS JOB:

- Lead Project Manager
- Operations Manager

KEY RESPONSIBILITIES:

- Building a staff team local to your region
- Managing business performance in your region
- Overseeing your company's go-to-market plan

KEY REQUIREMENTS:

- 5+ years in project or operations management
- 2+ years leading a team
- Expert understanding of the market you're expanding into

Don't like this job?
Try page 50

Like this job?
Try page 73

May require a college degree

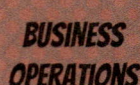

BUSINESS OPERATIONS

CONTINUE TO SOFTWARE AND TECH

SOFTWARE AND TECH

I've always been interested in tech and first got into esports after building my own PC. I know computer science is a good degree topic to choose because of the career prospects, but do those also exist in esports?

You're right, people who can code are in high demand across all industries right now. Is esports the same? Well, let's think about it. This is a digital industry that we follow through streaming services, websites and apps. These all need to be programmed by someone, so there are absolutely tech jobs available in esports.

Yeah, I mean there's software involved in almost every aspect of my life. It makes sense that esports is the same!

Now you're getting it! There are lots of lucrative career choices in tech that still allow you to contribute to the esports industry. Let's go through some of them now…

CONTINUE TO JOBS 68-79

WEB DEVELOPER

As a Web Developer, you'll be responsible for designing and building the visuals of a website. You'll have one foot in web design and the other in programming, which makes this role ideal if you enjoy both sides of development. Part of your job will consist of constructing wireframes, which are visual guides of how a web page will look, while the other part will have you laying the code to power them. If you're as comfortable on Photoshop or Figma as you are in HTML, then this might be a good fit for you.

EXPERIENCE LEVEL:

Entry   Junior   Inter.   Senior

ROLES THIS JOB COULD UNLOCK:

- Frontend Engineer
- UI Designer

ADDITIONAL RESOURCE:

SCAN ME

ROLES THAT LEAD INTO THIS JOB:

- Freelance Developer
- Junior Developer

KEY RESPONSIBILITIES:

- Conceptualizing web page layouts with UI designers
- Optimizing user experience by following best design practices
- Writing clean, functional code

KEY REQUIREMENTS:

- 1+ years writing frontend code
- 1+ years in graphic or UI design
- Fluency in frontend programming languages and design software

Don't like this job?
Try page 88

Like this job?
Try page 33

May require a college degree

SOFTWARE & TECH

UI DESIGNER

As a UI Designer, you'll be responsible for designing the visual experience of a website or app. After understanding what a page needs to include, you'll construct wireframes that lay these out in a user-friendly way. Wireframes are digital sketches of how a web page will look. You won't typically need any coding ability at all in this role; you'll be judged on your design skills instead. As such, mastery of a tool like Photoshop or Figma is essential, as is a portfolio of work that showcases a range of web page designs.

EXPERIENCE LEVEL:

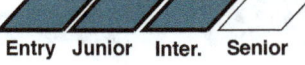

Entry   Junior   Inter.   Senior

ROLES THIS JOB COULD UNLOCK:

- Head of Design
- Head of User Experience

ADDITIONAL RESOURCE:

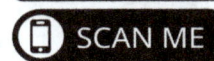

ROLES THAT LEAD INTO THIS JOB:

- Graphic Designer
- Junior UI Artist

KEY RESPONSIBILITIES:

- Building style guides to keep designs consistent
- Developing wireframes for developers to implement
- Working with the product team to understand what each page needs

KEY REQUIREMENTS:

- 2+ years in graphic or UI design
- A portfolio that features a variety of web page or app designs
- Knowledge of user experience best practices

**Don't like this job?
Try page 83**

**Like this job?
Try page 23**

May require a college degree

103

QA ANALYST

As a QA Analyst, you'll be responsible for testing new software before it launches. You'll be looking out for bugs, inconsistencies and anything that wasn't intended to be in the release. This could mean repeating the same action in a piece of software tens of times over, each with a slight alteration to cover all scenarios of how a user might interact with it. Technical skills are crucial here, followed by clear written communication. After spotting a bug, it's important that you outline how your developers can recreate the error. This is often an entry level or junior job, making it a great way for younger candidates to get started in the software field.

EXPERIENCE LEVEL:

Entry   Junior   Inter.   Senior

ROLES THIS JOB COULD UNLOCK:

- Backend Engineer
- Head of QA

ADDITIONAL RESOURCE:

 SCAN ME

ROLES THAT LEAD INTO THIS JOB:

- QA Intern
- Tech Support Specialist

KEY RESPONSIBILITIES:

- Building testing environments to identify potential bugs
- Reporting issues found to the development team
- Testing product features before they're released

KEY REQUIREMENTS:

- An interest in software and technology
- Clear communication skills
- Exceptional attention to detail

Don't like this job?
Try page 48

Like this job?
Try page 91

May require a college degree

SOFTWARE & TECH

UX RESEARCHER

As a UX Researcher, you'll be responsible for studying how users engage with your company's product. You'll perform quantitative analysis to learn where users spend the most time on a website or app and what behavior encourages them to make purchases. You will also perform qualitative research to capture feedback directly from users. A good UX researcher will be analytical, experienced with data analysis and able to significantly improve how a product is built by understanding how users interact with it.

EXPERIENCE LEVEL:

Entry   Junior   Inter.   Senior

ROLES THIS JOB COULD UNLOCK:

- Head of Product
- Head of Research

ADDITIONAL RESOURCE:

 SCAN ME

ROLES THAT LEAD INTO THIS JOB:

- Data Analyst
- Junior Researcher

KEY RESPONSIBILITIES:

- Conducting surveys, interviews and studies to capture user feedback
- Gathering actionable insights that can shape product decisions
- Setting up tracking to study user behavior

KEY REQUIREMENTS:

- 2+ years performing user research
- Bachelor's degree in psychology a plus
- Experience collecting data and presenting it clearly

Don't like this job? Try page 27

Like this job? Try page 94

May require a college degree

SOFTWARE & TECH

105

APP DEVELOPER

As an App Developer, you'll be responsible for developing and maintaining a mobile app. Depending on the role, you might be working on an app from scratch or joining a team mid-development. A key distinction between this role and other software development positions is that you'll usually need to work across both the iOS and Android operating systems. Each uses a different programming language, so it'll be your job to replicate the app as closely as possible on both device types. You'll also play a key role in the app's design, so understanding user experience fundamentals is essential.

EXPERIENCE LEVEL:

ROLES THIS JOB COULD UNLOCK:

- Engineering Manager
- Senior App Developer

ROLES THAT LEAD INTO THIS JOB:

- Freelance Developer
- Junior App Developer

KEY RESPONSIBILITIES:

- Designing an app's layout and key features
- Maintaining the app post-launch with updates and bug fixes
- Pushing new features and quality-of-life upgrades over time

KEY REQUIREMENTS:

- 1+ years in app development
- Ability to prioritize user experience in design
- Fluency in Swift (iOS) and Kotlin (Android) programming languages

Entry   Junior   Inter.   Senior

ADDITIONAL RESOURCE:

 SCAN ME

Don't like this job?
Try page 90

Like this job?
Try page 102

May require a college degree

SOFTWARE & TECH

TECH SUPPORT SPECIALIST

As a Tech Support Specialist, you'll be responsible for assisting employees or customers with their IT questions. If your company sells a technical product, then customers will expect help to be available when it goes wrong. And in companies with a large headcount, new hires will need assistance getting workstations set up. Whatever your focus is, the requirements are the same: you'll need expert IT knowledge and to be capable of fixing errors in hardware, operating systems and pieces of software. This is a junior position that's frequently offered on a remote basis, meaning it can be an accessible route into esports.

EXPERIENCE LEVEL:

Entry   Junior   Inter.   Senior

ROLES THIS JOB COULD UNLOCK:

- Head of Customer Support
- IT Manager

ADDITIONAL RESOURCE:

SCAN ME

ROLES THAT LEAD INTO THIS JOB:

- Customer Service Representative
- IT Assistant

KEY RESPONSIBILITIES:

- Resolving tech issues for employees or customers
- Setting up workstations and email accounts
- Working to fix any problems that arise as quickly as possible

KEY REQUIREMENTS:

- 1+ years in IT
- Expert knowledge of Windows, Linux and macOS
- In-depth knowledge of computer hardware or your company's products

Don't like this job?
Try page 128

Like this job?
Try page 82

May require a college degree

SOFTWARE & TECH

DEVOPS ENGINEER

As a DevOps Engineer, you'll be responsible for deploying and maintaining software systems. This is a varied role, so you might be building automated tools for your team to use one week and maintaining servers the next. A good devops engineer will have a grounding across software development, IT, databases and cloud engineering. A computer science degree will help you enter this career path, after which most people go into a junior devops position and build their experience there.

EXPERIENCE LEVEL:

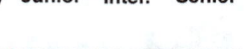

Entry   Junior   Inter.   Senior

ROLES THIS JOB COULD UNLOCK:
- Engineering Manager
- Senior Server Engineer

ADDITIONAL RESOURCE:

 SCAN ME

ROLES THAT LEAD INTO THIS JOB:
- Automation Engineer
- Release Manager

KEY RESPONSIBILITIES:
- Deploying cloud solutions and database updates
- Maintaining company servers and keeping them stable
- Managing network security and preventing website downtime

KEY REQUIREMENTS:
- 2+ years of software development experience
- 2+ years working with databases and web servers
- In-depth knowledge of network security and cloud engineering

**Don't like this job?
Try page 13**

**Like this job?
Try page 111**

May require a college degree

SOFTWARE & TECH

FRONTEND ENGINEER

As a Frontend Engineer, you'll be responsible for developing visible features on a website or piece of software. Above all, the systems you develop must prioritize user experience. You might do this by introducing tools and frontend widgets that make navigating your product seamless. Many developers are self-taught, so while a college degree will support your applications in this role it can usually be substituted for equivalent experience or personal projects. Anyone interested in this role should learn frontend programming languages like HTML, CSS and JavaScript.

EXPERIENCE LEVEL:

Entry   Junior   Inter.   Senior

ROLES THIS JOB COULD UNLOCK:

- Engineering Manager
- Senior Frontend Engineer

ADDITIONAL RESOURCE:

 SCAN ME

ROLES THAT LEAD INTO THIS JOB:

- Freelance Developer
- Junior Developer

KEY RESPONSIBILITIES:

- Developing new frontend features to improve user experience
- Listening to suggestions from stakeholders on new feature ideas
- Participating in code reviews

KEY REQUIREMENTS:

- 2+ years writing frontend code
- A portfolio of development projects on GitHub or similar
- Fluency in frontend programming languages

Don't like this job?
Try page 47

Like this job?
Try page 113

May require a college degree

SOFTWARE & TECH

109

BACKEND ENGINEER

As a Backend Engineer, you'll be responsible for building the functionality of a piece of software. This ranges from the nuts-and-bolts features needed to power a website like user logins and form submissions, to improving page load speed and reliability. Many developers are self-taught, so while a college degree will support your applications in this role it can usually be substituted for equivalent experience or personal projects. Anyone interested in this role should learn backend programming languages like Python, Java and Go.

EXPERIENCE LEVEL:

Entry | Junior | Inter. | Senior

ROLES THIS JOB COULD UNLOCK:

- Engineering Manager
- Senior Backend Engineer

ROLES THAT LEAD INTO THIS JOB:

- Freelance Developer
- Junior Developer

ADDITIONAL RESOURCE:

SCAN ME

KEY RESPONSIBILITIES:

- Developing new website and software functionality
- Optimizing your code for speed and stability
- Participating in code reviews

KEY REQUIREMENTS:

- 2+ years writing backend code
- A portfolio of development projects on GitHub or similar
- Fluency in backend programming languages

Don't like this job?
Try page 28

Like this job?
Try page 113

May require a college degree

SOFTWARE & TECH

SOFTWARE DELIVERY MANAGER

As a Software Delivery Manager, you'll be responsible for coordinating the development of a new piece of software. You'll utilize project management tools like JIRA to assign tasks, monitor workflows and track progress. This is a project management job, but requires candidates to have knowledge of software development so they can accurately predict timelines and communicate with engineers effectively. As such, you'll need to bring a blend of software development experience and a track record of managing projects to qualify for this role.

EXPERIENCE LEVEL:

Entry **Junior** **Inter.** **Senior**

ROLES THIS JOB COULD UNLOCK:

- Chief Product Officer
- Senior Project Manager

ADDITIONAL RESOURCE:

 SCAN ME

ROLES THAT LEAD INTO THIS JOB:

- Product Manager
- Project Manager

KEY RESPONSIBILITIES:

- Assigning and managing tasks through JIRA, Asana or a similar tool
- Helping resolve development roadblocks as they come up
- Keeping the team on-task, productive and aligned on vision

KEY REQUIREMENTS:

- 2+ years in project management
- 2+ years leading a team
- In-depth understanding of software development

Don't like this job?
Try page 71

Like this job?
Try page 98

May require a college degree

SOFTWARE & TECH

AI ENGINEER

As an AI Engineer, you'll be responsible for utilizing machine learning in your company's products. This job is most commonly hired for by software companies and startups, where you'll join the development team and use AI to help solve their problems. One common way that machine learning is used nowadays is through enhancing a feed of results based on how much a person has interacted with the content they've seen — like on popular social media apps. If you're a talented developer with a deep interest in how technology can be used, this could be a role for you to consider.

EXPERIENCE LEVEL:

Entry   Junior   Inter.   Senior

ROLES THIS JOB COULD UNLOCK:

- Head of AI
- Senior AI Engineer

ROLES THAT LEAD INTO THIS JOB:

- Backend Engineer
- Machine Learning Intern

KEY RESPONSIBILITIES:

- Building machine learning algorithms
- Participating in code reviews
- Using AI to solve business problems

KEY REQUIREMENTS:

- 2+ years in software development
- 2+ years using machine learning in code
- Excellent math and problem-solving skills

ADDITIONAL RESOURCE:

SCAN ME

 Don't like this job?
Try page 65

 Like this job?
Try page 137

 May require a college degree

SOFTWARE & TECH

ENGINEERING MANAGER

As an Engineering Manager, you'll be responsible for leading a team of software engineers on a project. This role focuses on the day-to-day management of your team, from setting tasks to conducting code reviews for junior developers. Mentorship is a key part of this role, as you'll be the most senior developer on a team. You'll regularly communicate with your engineers to keep them updated on feature priority and any changes that have come about to the project. To be successful in this job, you'll need extensive experience in software development and at least a few years in team management.

EXPERIENCE LEVEL:

Entry	Junior	Inter.	Senior
			■

ROLES THIS JOB COULD UNLOCK:

- CTO
- Head of Engineering

ADDITIONAL RESOURCE:

ROLES THAT LEAD INTO THIS JOB:

- Senior Backend Engineer
- Senior Frontend Engineer

KEY RESPONSIBILITIES:

- Establishing coding practices for your department to follow
- Leading a team of engineers on a development project
- Mentoring junior developers through code reviews

KEY REQUIREMENTS:

- 5+ years of software development experience
- 2+ years in team management
- Able to act as an engineering thought leader for your team

Don't like this job? Try page 131

Like this job? Try page 137

May require a college degree

SOFTWARE & TECH

CLIENT SERVICES

I was thinking the other day about how much of my free time I spend watching online content creators. For me, the personalities in esports are just as entertaining as the tournaments.

You're not alone in that! Esports is a form of competition and entertainment. While some people follow the top teams avidly, there are just as many who enjoy following influencers and streamers. It all depends on what you like.

So if esports is about entertainment as well, does that mean professional players are treated like celebrities? Do they have managers and agents?

That's right! Like the entertainment industry, esports has a number of agencies that provide services to players, influencers and other businesses. Why don't we learn about some of the agency jobs that support the industry…

ONTINUE TO JOBS 80-89

CAMPAIGN MANAGER

As a Campaign Manager, you'll be responsible for developing marketing campaigns on behalf of clients. These will often be coordinated over several avenues including social media, influencers and paid advertising. After receiving a brief from your client, you'll work to communicate their message to their target audience by selecting the right channels to advertise on. Once the campaign is finished, you'll report its effectiveness to the client and highlight key metrics. You'll need to bring customer service and marketing skills to the table here since you'll regularly be interfacing with clients.

EXPERIENCE LEVEL:

Entry   Junior   Inter.   Senior

ROLES THIS JOB COULD UNLOCK:

- Head of Marketing
- Senior Creative Strategist

ADDITIONAL RESOURCE:

 SCAN ME

ROLES THAT LEAD INTO THIS JOB:

- Marketing Coordinator
- Social Media Manager

KEY RESPONSIBILITIES:

- Building marketing campaigns that achieve a client's goal
- Priming influencers, media outlets and others to amplify a campaign
- Sending regular campaign updates to the client

KEY REQUIREMENTS:

- 1+ years working in social media
- 1+ years working in talent or digital marketing
- Creative thinker with endemic knowledge of esports

Don't like this job?
Try page 88

Like this job?
Try page 29

May require a college degree

CLIENT SERVICES

INFLUENCER MANAGER

As an Influencer Manager, you'll be responsible for coordinating brand activations with streamers and content creators on behalf of an agency. Candidates in this role will represent a network of talent and match their influencers to suitable campaigns. Part of your job will be to build a relationship with the talent you manage and understand their brand. On the flip side, you'll be speaking to brands to lock down deals for your talent. It's important to hold an up-to-date understanding of the creator landscape, too, so you can sign promising new influencers to your agency.

EXPERIENCE LEVEL:

Entry   Junior   Inter.   Senior

ROLES THIS JOB COULD UNLOCK:

- Head of Talent
- Marketing Manager

ADDITIONAL RESOURCE:

 SCAN ME

ROLES THAT LEAD INTO THIS JOB:

- Junior Marketing Manager
- Streamer

KEY RESPONSIBILITIES:

- Coordinating the planning & execution of an influencer campaign
- Managing a roster of influencers
- Sourcing brand deals for the talent you represent

KEY REQUIREMENTS:

- Account management or customer success experience
- Digital expert across streaming platforms and social media
- Prior experience as a streamer or content creator a plus

Don't like this job?
Try page 12

Like this job?
Try page 62

May require a college degree

CLIENT SERVICES

ACCOUNT EXECUTIVE

As an Account Executive, you'll be responsible for your agency's relationships with new and existing clients. You'll be in regular contact with the companies under your umbrella to pitch new ideas, campaign possibilities and to maintain an understanding of their marketing goals. You'll also approach new companies to win their business. This is a customer-facing role, so providing excellent client service is priority one. To qualify, you'll need a background in sales or business development along with an understanding of digital media.

EXPERIENCE LEVEL:

Entry   Junior   Inter.   Senior

ROLES THIS JOB COULD UNLOCK:

- Account Director
- Client Success Manager

ADDITIONAL RESOURCE:

 SCAN ME

ROLES THAT LEAD INTO THIS JOB:

- Business Development Associate
- Customer Service Representative

KEY RESPONSIBILITIES:

- Building case studies and other sales documents for clients
- Managing existing client relationships
- Pitching your agency's services to potential clients

KEY REQUIREMENTS:

- 1+ years in business development
- 1+ years in sales or digital marketing
- Excellent customer service skills

Don't like this job? Try page 61

Like this job? Try page 89

May require a college degree

CLIENT SERVICES

CLIENT SUCCESS MANAGER

As a Client Success Manager, you'll be responsible for providing an unbeatable experience for your company's clients. Think of yourself as the customer-facing part of an agency: you'll be on hand to answer a client's queries and regularly update them on their campaign's performance. This will take the form of project-managing deliverables with your team, compiling performance reports and passing client feedback onto your colleagues. Relationship-building skills are key here, so anyone interested in this field should look to build experience in sales or business development.

EXPERIENCE LEVEL:

Entry   Junior   Inter.   Senior

ROLES THIS JOB COULD UNLOCK:

- Account Director
- Account Executive

ADDITIONAL RESOURCE:

 SCAN ME

ROLES THAT LEAD INTO THIS JOB:

- Business Development Associate
- Junior Account Manager

KEY RESPONSIBILITIES:

- Acting as a bridge between your clients and colleagues
- Generating campaign reports
- Supporting team members to ensure campaign deliverables are met

KEY REQUIREMENTS:

- 1+ years in business development or sales
- 1+ years in marketing or online media
- Outstanding communication and presentation skills

 Don't like this job?
Try page 49

 Like this job?
Try page 86

 May require a college degree

 CLIENT SERVICES

COMMS STRATEGIST

As a Communications Strategist, you'll be responsible for working with media outlets on behalf of your agency's clients. Your main goal will be to generate news coverage about your client's activities, which could range from new hires to product launches to event recaps. As such, being well-connected in online media is a key requirement of this role — to the point where many comms professionals are former journalists themselves. A good communications strategist has excellent storytelling ability and can highlight what makes their client's news worth covering every time.

EXPERIENCE LEVEL:

Entry	Junior	Inter.	Senior

ROLES THIS JOB COULD UNLOCK:

- Communications Director
- Head of Communications

ROLES THAT LEAD INTO THIS JOB:

- Communications Coordinator
- Journalist

ADDITIONAL RESOURCE:

 SCAN ME

KEY RESPONSIBILITIES:

- Building media strategies for your clients to drive coverage
- Facilitating player and company interviews
- Writing and distributing press releases

KEY REQUIREMENTS:

- 1+ years in communications (agency experience preferable)
- Bachelor's degree in journalism or public relations a plus
- Outstanding written communication

Don't like this job?
Try page 102

Like this job?
Try page 41

May require a college degree

CLIENT SERVICES

TALENT AGENT

As a Talent Agent, you'll be responsible for the career management of content creators, on-air talent and professional players. Working under an agency, it's your mission to drive revenue for the people you represent, whether that's through brand deals or negotiating contracts on their behalf. An agent's commission is tied to the revenue they generate for clients, so it's important for anyone interested in this field to be entrepreneurial and motivated.

EXPERIENCE LEVEL:

Entry | Junior | Inter. | Senior

ROLES THIS JOB COULD UNLOCK:

- Head of Talent
- Senior Talent Agent

ADDITIONAL RESOURCE:

SCAN ME

ROLES THAT LEAD INTO THIS JOB:

- Professional Player
- Sponsorship Manager

KEY RESPONSIBILITIES:

- Meeting regularly with clients to develop their careers
- Negotiating contracts on behalf of clients
- Sourcing new revenue opportunities for clients

KEY REQUIREMENTS:

- A large network of contacts in esports
- Entrepreneurial background
- Previous experience at an agency a plus

 Don't like this job? Try page 71

 Like this job? Try page 30

 May require a college degree

 **CLIENT SERVICES**

121

CPC/SEM MANAGER

As a CPC/SEM Manager, you'll be responsible for running digital advertising campaigns on behalf of your agency's clients. This job focuses solely on paid campaigns — where brands pay for each impression, click or download they receive. You'll make sure that adverts of this type across social media, Google and ad networks are well-optimized for your clients. Most of your work will take place on channels like Google Ads and Twitter Ads. As such, experience in digital marketing where you'll be exposed to these programs can help you secure this role.

EXPERIENCE LEVEL:

Entry Junior Inter. Senior

ROLES THIS JOB COULD UNLOCK:

- Head of Digital Marketing
- Marketing Director

ROLES THAT LEAD INTO THIS JOB:

- Junior CPC Manager
- Junior SEM Manager

KEY RESPONSIBILITIES:

- Creating paid campaigns for socials, search engines and ad network
- Performing A/B tests to maximize performance
- Working with copywriters and designers to build compelling ads

KEY REQUIREMENTS:

- 2+ years building paid search/social campaigns
- Analytical, data-driven mindset
- Knowledge of ad exchanges and programmatic advertising

ADDITIONAL RESOURCE:

SCAN ME

Don't like this job?
Try page 22

Like this job?
Try page 33

May require a college degree

CLIENT SERVICES

CREATIVE STRATEGIST

As a Creative Strategist, you'll be responsible for defining the overall feel and vision of a client's campaign. You'll be the creative force behind your agency, taking client briefs and turning these into memorable advertising moments. This could be through designing visual assets for socials or storyboards for video shoots. Some of the key qualifiers for this role include past agency experience, a finger-on-the-pulse understanding of esports and a track record of building marketing strategies from scratch.

EXPERIENCE LEVEL:

Entry   Junior   Inter.   Senior

ROLES THIS JOB COULD UNLOCK:

- Creative Director
- Head of Strategy

ADDITIONAL RESOURCE:

SCAN ME

ROLES THAT LEAD INTO THIS JOB:

- Account Executive
- Campaign Manager

KEY RESPONSIBILITIES:

- Building concepts for advertising campaigns
- Creating a timeline for when different assets should be released
- Tailoring a campaign's approach to its target audience

KEY REQUIREMENTS:

- 3+ years in advertising (agency experience preferable)
- Authentic understanding of esports and its fanbase
- Excellent marketing fundamentals

Don't like this job? Try page 107

Like this job? Try page 41

May require a college degree

CLIENT SERVICES

123

ART DIRECTOR

As an Art Director, you'll be responsible for producing visual assets for your agency's clients. This will primarily be materials for client campaigns, such as social media graphics and advertising banners, but you'll also be assisting your sales team by creating pitch decks to attract new business. A key difference between this job and other graphic design roles is that, since you'll be working for an agency, everything you design must look appealing and drive conversions. As such, a background in advertising and visual design work best to unlock this role.

EXPERIENCE LEVEL:

Entry Junior Inter. **Senior**

ROLES THIS JOB COULD UNLOCK:

- Chief Creative Officer
- Creative Director

ADDITIONAL RESOURCE:

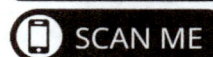
SCAN ME

ROLES THAT LEAD INTO THIS JOB:

- Graphic Designer
- Video Producer

KEY RESPONSIBILITIES:

- Building internal pitch decks and sales documents
- Leading a team of creatives to produce visual assets for clients
- Managing the approval of all assets before release

KEY REQUIREMENTS:

- 5+ years producing visual assets
- 1+ years leading a team
- High-level understanding of design, video editing and photography

Don't like this job?
Try page 82

Like this job?
Try page 34

May require a college degree

CLIENT SERVICES

ACCOUNT DIRECTOR

As an Account Director, you'll be responsible for two key tasks: managing your own set of clients (typically high-value ones) and supporting a team of account executives. As a senior staff member, you'll need to ensure high standards across your agency while supporting the career development of junior colleagues. This could be through defining workflows, building department guidelines and assisting teammates when they have questions. The most common route of entry for this role is by establishing yourself as an experienced account executive — typically with 5+ years in the field.

EXPERIENCE LEVEL:

| Entry | Junior | Inter. | Senior |

ROLES THIS JOB COULD UNLOCK:

- Head of Business Development
- Head of Client Services

ADDITIONAL RESOURCE:

SCAN ME

ROLES THAT LEAD INTO THIS JOB:

- Account Executive
- Client Success Manager

KEY RESPONSIBILITIES:

- Leading the day-to-day tasks of account executives
- Managing a small portfolio of your own clients
- Seeking out new business for your agency

KEY REQUIREMENTS:

- 5+ years in a marketing/client services agency
- 1+ years leading a team
- Expert in marketing, business development and customer service

Don't like this job?
Try page 66

Like this job?
Try page 98

May require a college degree

CLIENT SERVICES

125

HUMAN RESOURCES

When we first started talking about esports, I never imagined it would contain so many opportunities. I'm feeling more optimistic about the future, but if I'm honest I still don't know where I fit in.

That's a perfectly natural feeling to have — pursuing a career in a new industry can be scary. Fortunately, there's a group of people we haven't talked about yet whose job it is to support their colleagues in the workplace.

Great! I want all the options I can get. So, these people supporting their colleagues, how do they do that?

In a variety of ways. We're talking about human resources staff, and it's their job to make sure employees have a safe, fair and healthy work environment. They help build a positive company culture and look after staff members, among other things. Let's take a closer look at how they do that…

CONTINUE TO JOBS 90-95

HR COORDINATOR

As a HR Coordinator, you'll be responsible for supporting your company's present and future employees. This is often a varied role, which means you might be reviewing applications for a job opening one week and building an onboarding process the next. HR coordinators can also manage a company's benefits scheme and resolve workplace conflicts as they come up. This all requires a strong set of business skills. Chief among them are organization and communication, as you'll be the company's point-of-contact for many of your colleagues.

EXPERIENCE LEVEL:

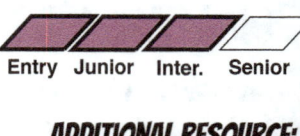

Entry   Junior   Inter.   Senior

ROLES THIS JOB COULD UNLOCK:

- HR Business Partner
- HR Director

ADDITIONAL RESOURCE:

 SCAN ME

ROLES THAT LEAD INTO THIS JOB:

- Administrative Assistant
- HR Intern

KEY RESPONSIBILITIES:

- Arranging company events and employee engagement activities
- Managing your company's benefit program
- Scheduling candidate interviews and defining onboarding practices

KEY REQUIREMENTS:

- 1+ years in human resources
- Bachelor's degree in human resources or similar
- Excellent communication skills and business sense

Don't like this job?
Try page 103

Like this job?
Try page 131

Requires a college degree

HUMAN RESOURCES

RECRUITER

As a Recruiter, you'll be responsible for sourcing candidates for your organization. Your main task is to network both in and outside of the esports community to find people who are the best in their field and attract them to your company. You'll also work with HR staff to assist with candidate interviews and understand which vacancies are the highest priority to fill at any given time. Some recruiters are specialists in a certain area, like tech or data analysis, in which case you'll need to have at least a basic understanding of that respective field.

EXPERIENCE LEVEL:

Entry | Junior | Inter. | Senior

ROLES THIS JOB COULD UNLOCK:
- Executive Recruiter
- HR Director

ADDITIONAL RESOURCE:

 SCAN ME

ROLES THAT LEAD INTO THIS JOB:
- HR Coordinator
- Talent Acquisition Coordinator

KEY RESPONSIBILITIES:
- Identifying potential hires for your organization
- Maintaining a network of talent to match your open roles with
- Providing a smooth candidate experience to all potential hires

KEY REQUIREMENTS:
- 2+ years in talent acquisition
- Being proactive in how you source talent
- Expertise in your area of recruitment (for specialists)

Don't like this job?
Try page30

Like this job?
Try page 83

Requires a college degree

HUMAN RESOURCES

DEI OFFICER

As a Diversity, Equity and Inclusion Officer, you'll be responsible for promoting fair, inclusive treatment in your organization and eliminating unconscious bias. You'll work to correct any company processes that unfairly impact underrepresented groups, such as poor hiring practices. Another focus of the job is on building diverse candidate pipelines, so you might be exploring where you can reach talent that your organization has struggled to access in the past. This role requires someone with experience in HR and a deep interest in DEI. Ultimately, your goal is to make everybody welcome at your company and combat workplace inequality.

EXPERIENCE LEVEL:

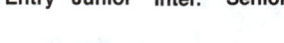

Entry   Junior   Inter.   Senior

ROLES THIS JOB COULD UNLOCK:

- Head of DEI
- Head of People

ADDITIONAL RESOURCE:

 SCAN ME

ROLES THAT LEAD INTO THIS JOB:

- HR Coordinator
- HR Manager

KEY RESPONSIBILITIES:

- Eliminating inequality in the workplace
- Ensuring all employees feel happy, safe and respected at work
- Identifying channels to source diverse applicants from

KEY REQUIREMENTS:

- 2+ years in human resources
- 1+ years in developing workplace programs
- A proven interest and care for DEI

Don't like this job?
Try page 70

Like this job?
Try page 133

May require a college degree

HUMAN RESOURCES

HR BUSINESS PARTNER

As a HR Business Partner, you'll be responsible for creating a great experience for your company's employees. You'll do this by understanding staff sentiment across the organization, feeding this back to department leaders and then developing programs that resolve the largest pain points. This is a senior role that requires candidates not only to have a background in human resources, but also business management and administration. A degree in organizational design, business management or human resources is usually required, too.

EXPERIENCE LEVEL:

Entry   Junior   Inter.   **Senior**

ROLES THIS JOB COULD UNLOCK:
- Head of People
- HR Director

ADDITIONAL RESOURCE:

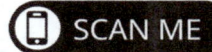 SCAN ME

ROLES THAT LEAD INTO THIS JOB:
- HR Coordinator
- HR Manager

KEY RESPONSIBILITIES:

- Building programs to improve employee experience
- Identifying organizational structures that could be improved
- Understanding employee satisfaction and working to raise this

KEY REQUIREMENTS:

- 5+ years in human resources
- Bachelor's degree in human resources, business administration or similar
- Highly organized and capable of leading programs independently

Don't like this job?
Try page 64

Like this job?
Try page 93

Requires a college degree

HUMAN RESOURCES

HR DIRECTOR

As a HR Director, you'll be responsible for managing the day-to-day operations of a company's human resources department. Alongside recruiters and HR coordinators, you'll implement a hiring strategy based on your company's goals, ensuring it's being run efficiently and on budget. You'll also support HR business partners as they work to drive changes across the company. As a managerial role, this will only be open to candidates with a significant amount of HR experience.

EXPERIENCE LEVEL:

Entry | Junior | Inter. | **Senior**

ROLES THIS JOB COULD UNLOCK:

- Chief People Officer
- Head of People

ADDITIONAL RESOURCE:

 SCAN ME

ROLES THAT LEAD INTO THIS JOB:

- HR Business Partner
- HR Manager

KEY RESPONSIBILITIES:

- Building learning and development programs for employees
- Managing HR policies, hiring strategy, onboarding & employee exits
- Performing staff evaluations on performance and wellbeing

KEY REQUIREMENTS:

- 5+ years in human resources
- 2+ years leading a team
- Deeply familiar with hiring, employment law and all HR functions

Don't like this job?
Try page 72

Like this job?
Try page 133

Requires a college degree

HUMAN RESOURCES

HEAD OF PEOPLE

As a Head of People, you'll be responsible for managing the overall strategy of a company's human resources department. More and more now, the term 'human resources' is being substituted for 'people' to reflect how this is the number one priority for HR staff. You will report directly to the CEO and help them implement HR strategies across the company, with your ultimate goal being to attract and retain the best talent around. As such, only senior business leaders with a proven track record in human resources will qualify for this role.

EXPERIENCE LEVEL:

Entry | Junior | Inter. | **Senior**

ROLES THIS JOB COULD UNLOCK:

- Chief Operating Officer
- Chief People Officer

ADDITIONAL RESOURCE:

SCAN ME

ROLES THAT LEAD INTO THIS JOB:

- HR Director
- Senior HR Business Partner

KEY RESPONSIBILITIES:

- Building a work environment capable of attracting top talent
- Hiring a HR department to support your goals
- Leading the HR team to develop processes for employee satisfaction

KEY REQUIREMENTS:

- 7+ years in human resources
- 3+ years leading a team
- Capable of being a HR thought leader among your organization

Don't like this job?
Try page 51

Like this job?
Try page 138

Requires a college degree

HUMAN RESOURCES

THE C-SUITE

This has been incredibly helpful! I feel like I have a much better grasp on all of the career opportunities in esports.

I'm glad to hear it, we've covered a lot of ground! I truly hope you have identified a route that interests you and have the information needed to prepare for that first job! Before we go, there is one final group of jobs we need to talk about – the C-Suite.

The C-Suite? What is that? It sounds like a fancy hotel room.

The C-Suite is a term referring to the executives that run a company. They are the highest level positions you can achieve and take a long time to reach. If you are building a career path and aiming to make it to the top, these would be the jobs to list as your end goal. Let's take a quick look at them…

CONTINUE TO JOBS 96-100

JOB #96 CHIEF OPERATING OFFICER

The COO is in charge of overseeing the day-to-day operations of an organization. They design processes for other departments to follow and usually serve as second-in-command at a company. As such, they work closely with the CEO to ensure all parts of the business are working towards their vision and operating efficiently.

JOB #97 CHIEF FINANCIAL OFFICER

The CFO oversees all of an organization's finances. They are in charge of the financial strength of a company and ensuring that it's either on the way to profitability or ensuring it stays there. They control all financial planning, risk assessments and legally-required statements.

JOB #98 CHIEF TECHNOLOGY OFFICER

The CTO is responsible for handling all of the technology that a company utilizes. This role can vary depending on the company type, but its main focus will always be on ensuring a business is using the most suitable technology for its needs and safeguarding the company's online presence. This can include overseeing IT infrastructure, networks and security, and managing software and storage services.

JOB #99 CHIEF REVENUE OFFICER

The CRO is in charge of generating revenue for the company. This can include sales, marketing, operations and client services. They will work closely with the COO to make sure operations are in place to successfully launch and grow new products, services and other revenue streams. They will also work with the CFO to understand the current financial load and what they need achieve to be cash-flow positive.

JOB #100 CHIEF EXECUTIVE OFFICER

The CEO is the leader of an organization. They are the visionary and the one who drives a company forward, building a capable team of staff around them as they go. In esports, the CEO is often the founder of the company and the one who built it from the ground up, though this isn't always the case. Sometimes CEOs can be brought in from outside of the industry or promoted through another C-Suite role.

YOUR FUTURE AWAITS...

FINAL STEPS

Hopefully you have a better idea of what your career path in esports could look like now. Please remember that learning about jobs is only the first step! It takes time to build the relevant skills—or learn the relevant programs—needed for the roles you're interested in.The more time you can dedicate to honing your skills now, the more likely you are to land the job you desire. And remember, you aren't alone in your job hunt. I'll always be here to help guide you. In fact, I'll go ahead and list your final steps to follow below—I'm confident they'll have you job hunting in no time!

1. For creative roles, like video editing, graphic design or similar, employers will want to see a portfolio. Now's the time to start working on that! You can begin with personal projects and work your way up to offering your services on websites like Fiverr. From there, every project you create helps strengthen your portfolio.

2. Once you're ready to start applying for jobs, you'll want to head to Hitmarker.net to begin your search. You'll also benefit from networking with as many people as possible in esports Discords and on Twitter to find out about opportunities and connect with potential hiring managers.

3. You'll need a strong resume to turn in each time you apply for a role. Luckily, we've already prepared everything you need to know. Give this article a read and refer to it as you structure your resume:

4. A unique cover letter is nearly always required in applications, too. Cover letters can be a little scary, but once more we've already prepared what you need to know! Just like the previous step, give this article a read and refer to it as needed.

5. Come back to this book whenever you feel stuck, lost or confused. We're rooting for you every step of the way!